Aelred of Rievaulx:
Pursuing Perfect Happiness

THE NEWMAN PRESS
SIGNIFICANT SCHOLARLY STUDIES

The Newman Press imprint offers scholarly studies in historical theology. It provides a forum for professional academics to address significant issues in the areas of biblical interpretation, patristics, and medieval and modern theology. This imprint also includes commentaries on major classical works in these fields, such as the acclaimed Ancient Christian Writers series, in order to contribute to a better understanding of critical questions raised in writings of enduring importance.

Aelred of Rievaulx: Pursuing Perfect Happiness

by

John R. Sommerfeldt

THE NEWMAN PRESS
New York/Mahwah, N.J.

Cover design by Cynthia Dunne

Book design by Celine M. Allen

The typeface used for chapter titles in this book is Clairvaux.

Library of Congress Cataloging-in-Publication Data

Sommerfeldt, John R.
   Aelred of Rievaulx : pursuing perfect happiness / by John R. Sommerfeldt.
      p.   cm.
   Includes bibliographical references and index.
   ISBN 0-8091-4261-9 (alk. paper)
   1. Aelred, of Rievaulx, Saint, 1110–1167. 2. Perfection—Religious aspects—
Catholic Church. 3. Happiness—Religious aspects—Catholic Church. I. Title.
   BX2350.5.S66 2005
   241'.042'092—dc22

                                                                    2004028977

Published by
THE NEWMAN PRESS
An imprint of Paulist Press
997 Macarthur Boulevard
Mahwah, New Jersey 07430

www.paulistpress.com

Printed and bound in the United States of America

Contents

This volume is dedicated to

CHRYSOGONUS WADDELL

monk of Gethsemani Abbey,
the most saintly of Cistercian scholars,
and
a dear friend of four generations
of Sommerfeldts

Table of Abbreviations

General Abbreviations

CCCM 1   *Corpus Christianorum Continuatio Mediaevalis*, I, *Aelredi Rievallensis Opera omnia, 1, Opera ascetica*. Ed. A. Hoste and C. H. Talbot. Turnholti: Typographi Brepols Editores Pontificii, 1971.

CCCM 2A   *Corpus Christianorum Continuatio Mediaevalis*, IIA, *Aelredi Rievallensis Opera omnia, Sermones I–XLVI*. Ed. Gaetano Raciti. Turnholti: Typographi Brepols Editores Pontificii, 1989.

CCCM 2B   *Corpus Christianorum Continuatio Mediaevalis*, IIB, *Aelredi Rievallensis Opera omnia, Sermones XLVII–LXXXIV*. Ed. Gaetano Raciti. Turnhout: Brepols Publishers, 2001.

CF   Cistercian Fathers series. Spencer, Massachusetts; Washington, DC; Kalamazoo, Michigan: Cistercian Publications, 1970–.

Cîteaux   *Cîteaux in de Nederlanden; Cîteaux: Commentarii cistercienses*, 1950–.

Coll   *Collectanea o.c.r.; Collectanea Cisterciensia*, 1934–.

CS   Cistercian Studies series. Spencer, Massachusetts; Washington, DC; Kalamazoo, Michigan: Cistercian Publications, 1969–.

CSQ   *Cistercian Studies* [periodical]; *Cistercian Studies Quarterly*, 1961–.

Historians 5   *The Historians of Scotland* 5. Edinburgh: Edmonston and
                    Douglas, 1874.

Lives   *Pinkerton's Lives of the Scottish Saints.* Ed. W. M. Metcalfe.
                    Paisley: Alexander Gardner, 2 vols., 1889.

PL   *Patrologia latina.* Ed. J.-P. Migne. Paris: apud J.-P. Migne
                    editorem, 221 vols., 1841.

Raine   James Raine, ed. *The Priory of Hexham: Its Chronicles,
                    Endowments and Annals* 1. Surtees Society 44. Durham:
                    Andrews & Co., 1863–1864.

RB   *Regula monachorum sancti Benedicti.*

SBOp   *Sancti Bernardi opera.* Ed. Jean Leclercq et al. Romae:
                    Editiones Cisterciensis, 8 vols. in 9, 1957–1977.

Works of Aelred of Rievaulx

Adv   *Sermo in adventu Domini*

Anima   *De anima*

Ann   *Sermo in annuntiatione Domini*

Ann dom   *Sermo in annunciatione dominica*

App   *Sermo in apparitione Domini*

Asc   *Sermo in ascensione Domini*

Asspt   *Sermo in assumptione sanctae Mariae*

Bello stand   *De bello standardii*

Ben   *Sermo in festo sancti Benedicti; sermo de sancto Benedicto;
                    sermo in festivitate beati Benedicti abbatis*

Cler   *Sermo ad clerum in synodo Trecensi*

Eul   *Eulogium Davidis regis Scotorum*

Gen Angl   *Genealogia regum Anglorum*

HM   *Sermo in hebdomada sancta*

Ie	*Sermo de ieiunio; sermo in capite ieiunii*
Iesu	*De Iesu puero duodenni*
Inst incl	*De institutione inclusarum*
Kal Nov	*Sermo in dominica in kalendis Novembris*
Nat	*Sermo in nativitate Domini*
Nat Ben	*Sermo in natali sancti Benedicti*
Nat JB	*Sermo in nativitate Ioannis Baptistae*
Nat M	*Sermo in nativitate sanctae Mariae*
Nat PP	*Sermo in natali sanctorum apostolorum Petri et Pauli*
Oner	*Sermo de oneribus*
Orat past	*Oratio pastoralis*
OS	*Sermo in festivitate omnium sanctorum; sermo in festo sanctorum omnium*
Palm	*Sermo in ramis palmarum*
Pasc	*Sermo in die pasco; sermo in sancto paschae*
Pent	*Sermo in die pentecostes*
PP	*Sermo in festivitate apostolorum Petri et Pauli*
Pur	*Sermo in purificatione sanctae Mariae*
Sanct Watt	*De sanctimonali de Watton*
Spec car	*De speculo caritatis*
Spir amic	*De spirituali amicitia*
SS Hag	*De sanctis ecclesiae Hagulstadensis*
Syn pres	*Sermo in synodo ad presbyteros*
Vita E	*Vita sancti Eduardi regis et confessoris*
Vita N	*Vita sancti Niniani*
Yp	*Sermo in ypapanti Domini*

Biblical Abbreviations

Ac	Acts
1 Cor	1 Corinthians
2 Cor	2 Corinthians
Dt	Deuteronomy
Eph	Ephesians
Ex	Exodus
Ezr	Ezra
Gal	Galatians
Gn	Genesis
Heb	Hebrews
Hos	Hosea
Is	Isaiah
Jas	James
Jb	Job
Jer	Jeremiah
Jn	John
1 Jn	1 John
1 K	1 Kings
2 K	2 Kings
Lam	Lamentations
Lk	Luke
Lv	Leviticus
Mk	Mark
Mt	Matthew
1 Pt	1 Peter
Phil	Philippians

Prv	Proverbs
Ps	Psalm
Qo	Ecclesiastes; Qoheleth
Rom	Romans
Rv	Revelation
Sg	Song of Songs
Si	Ecclesiasticus; Sirach
2 Sm	2 Samuel
Ti	Titus
1 Tm	1 Timothy
2 Tm	2 Timothy
Ws	Wisdom

Preface

A book requires an author, and I have tried mightily to make Aelred the author of this book. Aelred's teachings are, I believe, best presented by him, for Aelred understands himself far better than any commentator could. And Aelred surely expresses his teaching far more eloquently than is possible for me. So my approach has been simple: to read all of Aelred's known works and arrange them according to the concerns that Aelred thinks most important. In short, I have attempted to avoid interposing my own thought between Aelred and those who wish to learn from or about him.

Aelred wrote, of course, in Latin, and he wrote very well in that language. His masterful prose is a challenge to any translator, and, since the translations in this volume are mine, I have had to face the challenge of rendering Aelred's magnificent prose into an English which not only accurately reflects Aelred's meaning but also makes that meaning accessible. I have tried to convey a sense of Aelred's style, though Aelred's rhetorical skills often make that task difficult. To offer but one example of the problem and my attempted response, I cite Aelred's penchant for alliteration. It has often been impossible to alliterate in English where Aelred does so in Latin. To compensate for this, I have often alliterated in English where Aelred's Latin does not, though I have striven mightily to be faithful in this to the meaning of Aelred's text.

The footnote citations of Aelred's sermons also involve decisions that should be explained. Aelred's sermons *On the Burdens of Isaiah* (Oner) can be, and have been, numbered in two ways. This disparity is the result of the history of the composition of those sermons. Aelred first explored the meaning of the burdens presented in the prophetic book (Isaiah 13–16) in a sermon for Advent sent to

Gilbert Foliot, bishop of London. Aelred's monks then asked him to develop his observations in an extended commentary, and he did so. Aelred's effort resulted in thirty-one sermons on the subject. When, in the nineteenth century, J.-P. Migne put together his magnificent collection of sources, the *Patrologia latina,* he mistakenly counted the Advent sermon on Isaiah as the first of the series of sermons *On the Burdens.* Thus Migne's collection contains thirty-two such sermons. I have opted to follow Migne's faulty numbering because his is the edition most readily accessible, but the reader should be aware that this numbering system is not universally followed.

Aelred's sermons for the feasts of the liturgical year present a different sort of problem. These sermons were edited by Gaetano Raciti and numbered by him according to their place in the various manuscript collections that served as the basis for his edition. Thus, the reader should be aware that a reference to, for example, Nat 29 does not signal a quotation from Aelred's twenty-ninth Christmas sermon.

There is another potential source of confusion—this time in the numbering of the biblical citations. Aelred used the Vulgate text of the Bible, and I have followed him in this. Only in the book of Psalms, I think, might this lead to some difficulty. Through Psalm 8, the numbering is the same as in the King James, Revised Standard, and other Protestant versions—as well as in the newer Catholic editions. From Psalm 10 to 112, one should add one number to those given. The Vulgate Psalm 113 is contained in Psalms 114 and 115 of the newer versions. The Vulgate 114–115 become 116; 116–145 become 117–146. Psalms 146 and 147 of the Vulgate version are contained in Psalm 147—and the rest have the same numbering.

Scholarship is always the product of a collective effort, and a legion of generous helpers have contributed to this volume. I cannot here name all the members of that legion, but a few deserve special mention.

Cistercian nuns and monks, many of whom have invited me to speak on Aelred at their monasteries, have reacted with characteristic generosity to my words and have kindly corrected what they have found wanting or in need of amplification. One house in particular has extended its hospitality to me over a time span now numbering decades. Thus I am especially indebted to and grateful to Abbot

Thomas X. Davis and the brothers of the Abbey of New Clairvaux in Vina, California. Those who have succeeded one another as librarian of that abbey have helped me immeasurably; and so sincere thanks are due to John-Baptist Porter, Francis Flaherty, and Peter Damian Spera.

Members of the community at the Abbey of Gethsemani, in Kentucky, have also been of great assistance. Abbot Timothy Kelly graciously extended permission to borrow an early and precious edition of Aelred's works. Pascal Phillips and Chrysogonus Waddell also helped my effort, the first by sending me a book I could not obtain elsewhere, the second by his sage advice.

Aelred scholars in North America and Europe have responded quickly and generously to my requests for bibliographic assistance. So many scholars have helped me in this that I cannot name them all, but I must single out the extraordinary efforts of David Bell, Pierre-André Burton, Marsha Dutton, and Daniel La Corte. Most of these —and many others—have shared their insights with me through papers read and conversations shared at the annual Kalamazoo Cistercian Conference.

Five generous colleagues have made my task easier and, sometimes, simply possible. Beatrice Beech, formerly librarian of the Institute of Cistercian Studies at Western Michigan University, made available a rare book I could not elsewhere obtain. Alice Puro, interlibrary loan librarian at the University of Dallas, spent considerable time and her consummate skill in locating books exotically titled and distantly located. Professor E. Rozanne Elder, the editorial director of Cistercian Publications, generously sent me copies of useful materials awaiting publication. Professor Francis Swietek, a splendid Latinist and my friend and colleague at the University of Dallas, saved me several times from infelicities in my translations of Aelred's works. Dr. Christopher Bellitto, academic editor at Paulist Press, has offered sage advice and a friendship that I treasure.

Many students in classes and seminars at Western Michigan University, Michigan State University, the University of Dallas, and the Anglican School of Theology have responded to my discussions of Aelred and have presented papers that have enriched my understanding of the abbot of Rievaulx. Here I would single out two of my students who have written more extended pieces on Aelred. I profited greatly from Tyrrell Hughes's master's thesis: *Ailred of Rievaulx: The Consistency of His Life and Writings with His Thought and His Profession as a Cistercian Monk*. My friend Daniel Marcel La Corte is the author of an as yet unpublished doctoral dissertation, *Images of Abbot and Monastic Community in the Thought of Aelred of Rievaulx*, in the writing of which I hope I was of some small help. I am proud of the work of both students and have gained from their insights.

The physical production of this book was ably—and sometimes heroically—accomplished by two talented ladies, Cathy Carol and Celine Allen. Cathy not only translated my poor penmanship into typescript but also corrected many of the errors, omissions, and infelicities in my manuscript. Celine works a special sort of wonderful magic as a copy editor and typesetter.

I cannot adequately express the depth of my gratitude to my wife, Patricia, for the support and sacrifice that made this volume possible. I know that I could not have written this book without the loving understanding which she has consistently shown.

John R. Sommerfeldt
University of Dallas

1

An Introduction to Aelred

Aelred was born about the year 1110, the son and grandson of married priests who possessed some wealth and considerable influence in the area surrounding their church at Hexham in Northumbria.[1] It is likely that Aelred's father, Eilaf, had him instructed in at least the rudiments of Latin letters. When Aelred was fourteen or fifteen, he was sent to the court of King David of Scotland (1124–1153), where he spent some nine years and where he deepened his knowledge of both Latin and vernacular literature. In the course of time, Aelred was appointed David's *echonomus,* serving, in all likelihood, as steward of the royal table.[2]

In 1134, King David sent Aelred on a mission to Archbishop Thurstan of York, who but two years before had assisted in the foundation of a new Cistercian monastery at Rievaulx in north Yorkshire. On the way back to the Scottish court, Aelred stopped to survey the new monastery,[3] and the next day he returned to commit himself to the life he found there.

In 1142, Aelred's abbot, William, formerly secretary to Saint Bernard at Clairvaux, entrusted the young monk with a mission to Rome. Aelred was to represent the Cistercian abbeys of Yorkshire in the controversy that had arisen over the election of one of King Stephen of England's kinsmen as archbishop of York. One supposes that the journey was interrupted by a stopover at Clairvaux, Rievaulx's mother house, and it is possible that Aelred then met its abbot, Bernard. Whether Bernard came to know Aelred then or at some other time, Bernard was sufficiently impressed by the young monk to send him a letter encouraging him to write a treatise on love,[4] an encouragement that later bore fruit in Aelred's first work, *The Mirror of Love*. Bernard's letter reached an Aelred now installed as master of Rievaulx's novices, a position he was to hold during the years 1142 and 1143. In the latter year, Abbot William selected Aelred to be the abbot of Rievaulx's new foundation at Revesby in Lincolnshire.

In 1147, when Aelred was about thirty-seven years old, he was recalled by the monks of Rievaulx to serve them as abbot, in which role he served until his death in January of 1167. Aelred's abbatiate saw the growth of his community from some three hundred monks[5] to perhaps more than six hundred.[6] In addition to his responsibility for all things spiritual and material[7] at Rievaulx, Aelred was obliged to attend the General Chapter, the annual meeting of all Cistercian abbots at Cîteaux, and to conduct an annual visitation of each of Rievaulx's five daughter houses.[8]

But Aelred's abbatial ministry was not confined to serving his own monastery or the Cistercian order of which it was a part. As an ecclesiastical figure of some prominence, and as a man increasingly well known for his spiritual insight, Aelred was often called on to exercise his eloquent counsel outside the cloister. Aelred's influence with King Henry II of England (1154–1189) was, some think, one of the major factors in the king's decision to support Pope Alexander III against the anti-pope Victor IV in the schism of 1159. Aelred also served as arbiter in several serious ecclesiastical disputes. The political tensions that plagued the border lands between England and Scotland also saw Aelred playing the role of peacemaker. He was often called on to preach at solemn ecclesiastical and political occasions—in England, Scotland, and on the continent—notably at the translation of the relics of Edward the Confessor. Aelred's many activities outside the cloister[9] have earned him the sobriquet "the Bernard of the North."[10]

Aelred also spent much of his energy and considerable rhetorical skills in composing sermons, letters,[11] treatises, and historical works. Marsha Dutton has written of these:

Aelred's works may be roughly grouped into historical and spiritual subjects, distinct in subject matter and audience. One may sometimes forget Aelred the spiritual director when reading Aelred the historian, while the spiritual treatises, which explore the way to God through love of humankind, seem timeless, ahistorical, as though written by someone without interest in events of the day.[12]

Yet even Aelred's historical works point the way to spiritual advancement. His *Eulogy* of 1155, mourning the recent death of the virtuous King David of Scotland, is aimed at inspiring the king's successor to imitate those virtues and influencing the Scots to continue their loyalty to virtuous rulers. Aelred's *Genealogy of the Kings of England* (1153–1154), *The Battle of the Standard* (1155),[13] and *Life of Saint Edward the Confessor* (1163) were all intended to foster in the powerful the virtuous conduct displayed in the events related. In a series of hagiographical works and miracle stories, Aelred placed before folk of all classes the virtues of the progenitors of the faith and contemporary saints in the lands of the Scots and English. These works include *The Life of Saint Ninian* (perhaps 1154–1160), *The Saints of Hexham* (begun, probably, in 1155), and *The Nun of Watton* (1158–1165).

Aelred's spiritual works, which are the source for most of what will be read in this volume, include *The Mirror of Love* (sometime after 1143), *On Jesus at the Age of Twelve* (1153–1157), and *On Reclusion* (1160–1166). Several collections of Aelred's sermons have also survived. These include his sermons *On the Burdens of Isaiah,* elaborations, requested by Aelred's monks, on a theme first explored in an Advent sermon he had sent to Gilbert Foliet, bishop of London. Aelred's obligation to preach to his monks on the principal feasts of the Cistercian liturgical calendar[14] resulted in sermon collections that have been edited by Gaetano Raciti[15] and C. H. Talbot.[16] Aelred's spiritual works also include two dialogues: *On the Soul* (1163–1166) and *On Spiritual Friendship* (1164–1167).

Aelred's health was, apparently, fragile throughout his life. The last ten years of his life brought him intense suffering from arthritis and severe attacks of pain from what seem to have been kidney stones. As early as 1157, the General Chapter of his order allowed Aelred to attend the daily liturgical celebrations of his monastery only when he felt up to the effort. Aelred's fellow abbots also allowed him to eat and sleep in Rievaulx's infirmary, where his monks built for him a place of private refuge. Aelred's biographer, Walter Daniel, relates how very little privacy Aelred was accorded:

> . . . Twenty or thirty of them would come there each day and talk about the spiritual delights found in Scripture and about the order's observance. There was no one to say to them: "Get out! Go away! Do not touch your abbot's bed!" Rather, walking or lying about his cot, they talked with him like a little child chats with its mother.[17]

Walter also relates that, on his deathbed, Aelred

> admonished us to bring him his glossed psalter, the *Confessions* of Augustine, and the text of John's gospel, along with the relics of some saints and a small cross which had belonged to Archbishop Henry of York. He said to us: "See, I have kept these with me in my little oratory. And I have delighted in them as I could when I have had time and leisure to sit alone in it. 'Silver and gold I have none [Ac 3:6],' so I make no will. Since I possess nothing of my own, whatever I have—and I myself—are yours."[18]

And so, in 1166, died the man who "wrote words of advice for the king of England, corresponded with kings, abbots, and bishops throughout Europe, and traveled, ruled, and adjucated, all the while guiding and building the monastery of which he was abbot to astounding size and prominence."[19] Though of great stature in the eyes of the world, Aelred died in the simplicity for which he had come to Rievaulx—a simplicity that he tried to teach his monks and that, perhaps, may be of some interest to those who read the pages that follow.

B. The Growth of Aelredian Scholarship

Aelred has not received the attention accorded to his friend and fellow-abbot, Bernard of Clairvaux. Indeed, it was not until the 1930s that Aelred began to be studied in any depth. The interest that began then has flowered in subsequent years, and this has resulted in the production of numerous critical editions, books, and articles—a flood of scholarship that shows no sign of diminishing.[20]

It is not surprising that significant contributions to that scholarship have been made by nuns and monks. Among the many significant contributors to this renewal of monastic interest,[21] two monk-scholars stand out, I believe; they are Charles Dumont and Amédée Hallier. Since the 1950s, Charles Dumont has aroused the enthusiasm of generations of Aelredian scholars through his prodigious and penetrating scholarship, shared primarily through a profusion of articles rather than a single work. On the other hand, Amédée Hallier's most profound influence has been through the publication, in 1959, of his doctoral dissertation, *Un Éducateur monastique: Aelred de Rievaulx*,[22] which soon appeared in English as *The Monastic Theology of Aelred of Rievaulx: An Experiential Theology*.[23] This work remains the necessary starting point for all serious students of Aelred's thought.

Scholars who were not monks also played a critical role in the initial and vital phases of the Aelredian revival. Among the most influential was Louis Bouyer, whose *La Spiritualité de Cîteaux* (1955; English translation 1958) contained a chapter on Aelred that was one of the most complete and penetrating expositions of Aelred's thought available at the time.[24] F. M. Powicke's intent was, instead, to explore the historical setting in which Aelred lived and acted. Powicke pursued this goal through a long series of articles, and one of his most valuable contributions has been the introduction to his edition and translation of Aelred's biography.[25] C. H. Talbot's contribution has been in the realm of literary studies, and, more generally, in intellectual history. His skill as a finder and reader of manuscripts has led to the critical editions of many of Aelred's sermons and treatises.[26] Another scholar, one who began his studies of Aelred in the 1950s, was Aelred Squire, a Dominican who died recently after having become, successively, a hermit in Norway and a Camaldolese monk. The most influential of his many contributions to Aelredian studies has been a revision of his 1958 Oxford dissertation, published in 1969 with the straightforward title *Aelred of Rievaulx: A Study,*[27] and now reprinted for the benefit of all who would pursue the study of Aelred's thought.[28]

Among the factors that led to the more recent continuation and intensification of Aelredian studies was the fact that many nuns and monks have found in Aelred a special relevance to the renewal of monastic life that followed the Second Vatican Council.[29] Basil Pennington, of St. Joseph's Abbey in Massachusetts, took seriously the council's admonition to all religious "to return to the sources,"[30] and almost immediately after the council began to produce and publish English translations of the works of all the early Cistercian authors. Thus he made those authors, including Aelred of course, available to a monastic audience that was increasingly unfamiliar with Latin. For this purpose he founded Cistercian Publications, which not only continues to publish those translations in its Cistercian Fathers series but also produces the Cistercian Studies series, an ever-expanding collection of significant commentaries on Cistercian authors, monographs, and collections of articles concerning all sorts of topics of interest to monastic (and now lay) audiences, as well as translations of patristic authors who influenced the early Cistercians. Father Basil soon discovered that this mammoth task was too much for one monk, and, at my invitation, he transferred the editorial offices of Cistercian Publications to the Institute of Cistercian Studies at Western Michigan University, an institute that I founded largely for this purpose. The work of Cistercian Publications continues under the capable direction of Professor E. Rozanne Elder, its editorial director and my successor as director of the Institute of Cistercian Studies. The Institute also sponsors an annual Cistercian Conference, held each year in May in conjunction with the International Medieval Congress in Kalamazoo, Michigan, sponsored by the Medieval Institute of Western Michigan University and capably hosted by my successors as director of that latter Institute, Otto Gründler and, now, Paul Szarmach. Thus the interest in Cistercian studies—and Aelredian studies—has been fostered and flourishes, not only for and through the contributions of many monks and nuns but also as a result of the studies of the legions of lay scholars concerned with Cistercian life and thought.

Lay folk, including scholars, were initially attracted to Aelred by the discovery of Aelred's teaching on friendship. This was really a rediscovery, for, as early as 1934, Bede Jarrett, a Dominican, had written with enthusiasm: "The beauty of his [Aelred's] life is the beauty of his friendships; for him they made his life, they helped him to understand life, they gave life the only value it had for him . . . ."[31] Appreciation of Aelred's teaching on friendship still motivates students of Aelred's thought. Recently, Bernard McGinn has written that Aelred's "*amicitia spiritualis* [spiritual friendship] takes its place alongside Bernard's *amor sponsalis* [bridal love] as the main contributions to the Cistercian mysticism of love."[32]

Two scholars have given important impetus to the increasing interest in Aelred's notion of friendship. One is Adele Fisk, who called attention to Aelred's teaching in an article in *Cîteaux*, "Aelred of Rievaulx's Idea of Friendship and Love,"[33] and in a monograph entitled *Friends and Friendship in the Monastic Tradition*,[34] which devoted thirty-one pages to Aelred. Charles Dumont has inspired enthusiasm for Aelred's insights into friendship in both the English- and the French-speaking worlds. Two examples of his scholarly yet eminently accessible works on this subject, one in each language, are: "Aelred of Rievaulx's *Spiritual Friendship*," published in the United States in 1978;[35] and "L'amour fraternel dans la doctrine d'Aelred de Rievaulx," published in Belgium in 1989.[36] In part because of the contributions of these scholars, but above all because of the attractive teaching of Aelred himself, Aelred's treatise *De spirituali amicitia* has been translated into Dutch, English (six times), French, German, Italian, and Spanish.[37] And, in Burton's recent bibliography, there are twenty-seven listings of works on Aelred's teaching on friendship.[38]

As interest in Aelred grew, so too did the range of topics to which scholars directed their attention. The works cited in the bibliography of this book give a small indication of the newfound excitement of the scholarly world with all aspects of Aelred's thought. That bibliography indicates my debt to the work of nuns and monks, such as Elizabeth Connor and Pierre-André Burton, and that of lay scholars, such as Marsha Dutton, Brian Patrick McGuire, and Thomas Renna, to name only a few. An encouraging sign for the continuing vitality of Aelredian studies is the number of theses and dissertations devoted to Aelred. In recent years, several universities of all sorts have produced Aelred scholars. Among those schools are the Catholic University of America (Katherine Yohe, née TePas), Fordham University (Daniel La Corte and Marie Anne Mayeski), Harvard University (Douglas Roby), The University of Michigan (Marsha Dutton), and Western Michigan University (my student Tyrrell Hughes).

Interest in Aelred has lately been stimulated by the publication, in 1980, of a book by John Eastburn Boswell entitled *Christianity, Social Tolerance, and Homosexuality: Gay People in Western Europe From the Beginning of the Christian Era to the Fourteenth Century*.[39] Boswell presents Aelred as a representative of medieval homosexuality (pp. 41–59), and the controversy that this thesis elicited has been heightened by the publication, in 1994, of Brian Patrick McGuire's *Brother and Lover: Aelred of Rievaulx*.[40] In this book McGuire attempts to convince the reader that Aelred was indeed a homosexual as Boswell had asserted, but with far greater detail than was possible in Boswell's more general work.

McGuire's book has been widely reviewed,[41] but two examples may serve to illustrate the widely divergent responses to it. Writing in *Speculum*, Thomas Bestul states:

> Although he [McGuire] consistently portrays Aelred as powerfully attracted to other males, he concludes that his sexual identity remains uncertain. The equivocation no doubt arises from the desire to be fair, coupled with a desire not to give offense. McGuire speaks warmly of his participation in the Cistercian sessions at Kalamazoo, and he seems to have the complete spectrum of that audience in mind as he writes. To me, we have more evidence about Aelred's sexuality than for most medieval figures, and John Boswell's discussion, now fifteen years old, remains balanced, direct, and persuasive. Nevertheless, McGuire is a refreshing alternative to those scholars who by insisting on the impossible standards of "proof" seem determined to save Aelred for heterosexuality at all costs.[42]

Although I know of no scholars who would "save Aelred for hetero-sexuality," it is surely true that some scholars have rejected McGuire's thesis on other grounds. Marsha Dutton has criticized McGuire's insis-tent affirmation of Aelred's homosexuality on the basis of what she sees as his faulty methodology, his factual inaccuracies, and his disre-gard for, or misinterpretation of, some of Aelred's writings. She has commented:

> Scholars who wish to construct a new political myth must not confuse their construction of such meaning with the work of disinterested scholarship, carried out in search for historical understanding. When such a projection of the con-cerns of the present upon the past ignores the reality of the past it denies readers the opportunity to evaluate the evi-dence for themselves, just as it denies authors their right to be fairly heard and fairly represented.[43]

In order to allow readers to evaluate the evidence for Aelred's posi-tion on sexuality, Dutton has assembled a vast array of Aelredian texts in an article entitled "Aelred of Rievaulx on Friendship, Chastity, and Sex: The Sources."[44] On the basis of this evidence, Dutton's answer to the question of Aelred's homosexuality is that "there is finally no way of knowing the details of Aelred's life, much less his sexual expe-rience or struggles."[45] She is surely right. But, still more relevant to Aelredian scholarship, she writes:

> The question of Aelred's sexuality is . . . the wrong question. . . . The question that must be asked is not "was Aelred gay" or "was Aelred a friend," just as it is not "was Aelred a mys-tic" or "did Aelred really admire King Henry." Rather, the question of importance for twentieth-century readers of the Cistercian Fathers is what Aelred has to say about spiritual friendship and the love of God. That is a question we can answer; that is a question of real meaning, importance, and personal value for all of us, gay or straight, male or female, married or single, Christian or Jew or Sufi.[46]

11
Adam's Wondrous Dignity

uman beings long for happiness, and human existence has happiness as its natural end—so Aelred of Rievaulx believes. To put this another way, the happiness for which humans long is the fulfillment of their nature as human beings. For Aelred, human beings are rational creatures created to participate in the happiness, the beatitude, of their loving Creator.[1] Thus, says Aelred, "we were created with the highest dignity...."[2] This dignity derives from the Creator in whose image humans are made—made in the creative act that is only the first of his many gifts to humankind. Throughout their lives, humans continue to be "surrounded on all sides by his [God's] innumerable favors."[3] Aelred likens the image and likeness conferred by God on humans to the tribute coin of Matthew 22:19–20: "God has stamped his image on the very nature of the rational soul...."[4] It is because of human participation in the nature of God, of a loving God, that human nature is good and capable of the happiness for which God created it. To be sure, humans share with all other creatures the derivative and dependent nature of their existence.[5] As rational beings, however, humans are given a greater share in God's being.[6]

All of this may sound rather abstract and remote. But the message assumes immediacy and existential relevance for Aelred when he considers the meaning of human nature, dignity, and dependence for his central concern, human happiness: "For, in the creation of all things, he [God] gave humans not only being and not only some good or beautiful or well-ordered being—as he gave to other creatures—but, beyond these, he granted humans happiness in being."[7] Human beings, then, are capable of happiness, and this is because human nature is good. For Aelred, the ultimate testimony to the goodness of human existence is the fact that the Second Person of the Trinity assumed human nature: "You know well, my brothers, that in our Lord Jesus Christ there are two natures, divine and human. These two natures are so perfect in him that his divine nature was not diminished on account of his humanity, nor was his human nature annihilated by his divinity."[8]

A. THE RATIONAL AND SOCIAL ANIMAL

Human nature is, thus, good and capable of the happiness for which God created it. But in what does human nature consist? What is the nature of these humans who have the capacity for happiness? The notion of happiness, of fulfillment, demands a description of the nature that is fulfilled. Aelred knows this, and he provides answers that are rich and multi-faceted.

"...A human being is composed of a body and of a soul...."[9] Aelred often repeats this seemingly straightforward and perhaps obvious analysis—sometimes in the first person: "...I [am] a human being, made up of body and soul...."[10] This is the "body and soul which the Son of God assumed"[11] in becoming human. And, for Aelred, this is the sum total of human nature; there is no other component.[12]

Though distinct, the body and the soul are essential components of human nature. The high level of awareness, the consciousness or, as Aelred puts it, the rationality of the soul and the corporeality of the body are both necessary to being human.[13] Aelred asserts that human beings are indeed animals; they are naturally physical. They are also rational: they perceive; they have awareness or consciousness. A human being is thus an entity; in humans, rationality, or consciousness, and physicality—or mortality, as Aelred sometimes puts it—are conjoined.[14]

That first creation also saw God's initiative in making humans social beings:

> ...When he [God] created [the first] human, in order to
> commend the goodness of society, he said: "It is not good

for the man to be alone; let us make for him a helper like himself [Gn 2:18]." It was from no similar stuff, nor even from the same matter that the divine power formed this helper. But, as a more pressing incentive to love and friendship, he brought forth the woman from the very substance of the man. How beautiful it is that the second human being was taken from the side of the first [see Gn 2:21–22], so that nature might teach that all [humans] are equal—side by side, so to speak—and that there might be no superior or inferior in human affairs . . . .[15]

Humans are thus, by their very nature, physical, rational, and social animals.

B. THE BEAUTIFUL BODY

The human body,[16] Aelred is sure, is composed of the same elements that make up the bodies of other animals—and, indeed, all of the material world: earth, air, water, and fire.[17] Despite the limitations of the human body,[18] it provides services essential to life as a human. And one of the foremost of these, for Aelred, is sensation, through which one "senses heat and cold, hardness and softness, lightness and heaviness, hardness and smoothness. Then it senses and perceives innumerable distinctions in colors, shapes, scents, tastes, and sounds by seeing, smelling, tasting, and hearing. [Thus] it seeks out those qualities that it finds agreeable and escapes those that it finds disagreeable."[19] The influx of sensation from the body provides information that enables one to direct and control the body.[20] Aelred quotes Augustine of Hippo to show how this dual motion of sensation and physical direction works:

"... From this [brain], as from a central point, delicate tubes lead not only to the eyes but also to the other sensors—to the ears as to the nostrils and the palate, for hearing, smelling, and tasting. The same is true of the sense of touch present in the whole body, said to be directed by the cerebrum through the cervical medulla and through [the nerve] contained by the spinal column, and thence diffused through each part [of the body] by means of the extremely fine channels which make up the sense of touch."[21]

The physiology of sensation may seem irrelevant to Aelred's concern for human happiness, but it is truly crucial to that concern—at least as Aelred sees it. For the body supplies through the senses the raw material for thought: "This happens through hearing, through taste, through smelling, through touch—all of which feed the soul with an array of thoughts when they have been presented...."[22] Thus knowledge of the whole of creation is made available to the human mind; thus "the images of things penetrate the soul by means of the senses...."[23] Aelred insists that "it is impossible to think about anything except through images of bodies which you have perceived by means of the senses, which you have [then] fashioned by imagining."[24]

For Aelred, the value of the human body is demonstrated unequivocally by the Incarnation. Jesus had a body subject to all of the needs and limitations of the flesh: "He hungered, thirsted, was sad; he wept, slept, was exhausted."[25] Aelred's, and all humans', physical limitations—infirmity and mortality—are part and parcel of the human condition that the Son shared. And corporeality was not a passing condition for the Son of God; after his death he continued and continues to exist in the flesh.[26]

As Aelred sees it, the human body goes through three stages in the course of salvation history: "In paradise the body can be called a body of happiness and of justice, in this life a body of sin and of unhappiness, in that beatitude a body of happiness and of glory. ...[For] our Lord had his flesh from the flesh of Adam, and...he came and restored the flesh of Adam to its pristine state...."[27] Thus, in its natural state the body is good; in its glorified state that goodness will be reaffirmed. Aelred rejects the notion that the body is a prison for the soul, as he understands some heretics affirm: "Since they do not believe in the resurrection of the body, perhaps the most impure demon has persuaded them that their bodies are their prisons, promising them ineffable bliss when they have been liberated from this dungeon."[28]

The ineffable bliss of the coming life will, rather, be with the flesh and in the body:

> We await perfect glory at our resurrection, when this mortal [nature] will clothe itself in immortality and this corruptible [body] will don incorruption [see 1 Cor 15:53], when "shall come to pass what is written: 'Death is devoured in victory [1 Cor 15:54; see Hos 13:14].'" And what will be the nature of this glory? Then in our body will be the perfection of health and beauty, of strength and swiftness . . . .[29]

All the troubles to which the flesh is heir will be ended in the coming perfection of the body,[30] which will also possess to perfection all its natural powers:

> It should not be believed that the resurrected body is without sensation or has some other form of sensation than that which now invigorates it. The human body will arise with all the perfection and integrity of its nature, but with all its corruption annihilated—this the Christian faith does not doubt. Why, then, should we not believe that the power of sensation and motion, having reverted [in death] to those elements from which it was made, will be taken up again, with the body, by the soul on the day of judgment?[31]

This restoration of the body and its powers to the soul awaits the end of earthly time, when Christ shall come again—a coming, Aelred reminds his hearers, in the body, "in the same flesh, in the same form, with the same scars and wounds which he carried with him to heaven."[32] Thus, for Aelred, Jesus' presence in heaven is even now a physical presence.

For Aelred, then, the body is good, the body's very limitations are natural and thus good, and the body will be perfected in the happiness of heaven. And so the death of the body brings no fears:

> It dies that it may be brought to life, dissolved that it may be restored still better. "Sown in weakness, it will arise with

power [1 Cor 15:43]." "Sown in corruption, it will arise in incorruption [1 Cor 15:42]." "Sown in dishonor, it will arise in glory [1 Cor 15:43]." Lastly, "sown an animal body, it will arise as spiritual [1 Cor 15:44]." "Death, where is your victory? Death, where is your sting? [1 Cor 15:55]."[33]

C. The Potent Soul

Human beings are not souls; they are creatures who have bodies and souls. Still, Aelred admonishes, one should "consider the great dignity of the rational soul."[34] He follows his own advice—above all in a treatise titled specifically *On the Soul*. There Aelred teaches that the soul is an incorporeal substance.[35] Indeed, as firmly as Aelred insists on the enduring physicality of the human being, he as strongly maintains the non-physical nature of the human soul: "The soul is not a body; it has no resemblance to a body. It is not [composed of] earth, air, water, or fire. . . . It does not have corporeal shape or form by which we can distinguish its nature with our eyes, hear with our ears, feel with our touch, sense with our smell, or discern with our taste."[36]

The reason the physical senses cannot discover, or examine, the soul is that the soul's essential operation, thought—its enduring characteristic, consciousness—is not susceptible of sensation.[37] The consciousness—the thought processes, the rationality—of the soul leads Aelred to "creep into a certain definition of the soul."[38] This "definition" quickly becomes a description:

> It seems to me that the human soul . . . is, in our present state, a form of rational life, mutable in time but not in place, immortal in its own way, and capable of happiness or wretchedness. In calling its life rational, I exclude precisely the life by which trees and cows live, for they are devoid of reason. By saying that it is temporally mutable, I [wish to] affirm that its nature is not that of God, which is not mutable in place or time. By saying that it is immortal in its own way, I exclude that immortality which the apostle says belongs only to the being of God, . . . [who] is always the same and exists in the

same way. This I cannot say of the soul, which is drawn here and there by its various desires and decisions.[39]

Though the soul's nature is not God's, it is made in God's image and likeness. To explain this, Aelred creates his own image of the creation of that image and likeness:

If you wish to paint a picture in the image and likeness of some person, you first outline the height and breadth of that person's parts and distinctive features—and thus you have an image of that person. And yet you will not have produced a likeness—at least not as close a likeness as is possible. Then, if you subtly apply various colors to this image—following the model sitting before you and in all ways re-presenting the beauty imaged—you will produce a picture made not only in the person's image but in his or her likeness. Thus we say that the rational soul is made, according to its nature or essence, in the image of God, and, according to its beauty— that is, its virtue—in the likeness of God.[40]

"There are three components comprising the nature of the rational soul," says Aelred, and "they are memory, reason, and will."[41] The triune nature of the soul is no accident, as Aelred sees it, for

these three are the substance of the soul, one simple, noncomposite life, which is made in the image of its Creator, who, though he is one God and one essence, is, nevertheless, Father and Son and Holy Spirit. These exist in such a way that there is with them no commixture of the three, no division, no separation from their unity. In the same way these three—memory, reason, and will—are both three and no less one.[42]

Because the soul is made in the image and likeness of God, it is able to discover him in itself,[43] and thus reflection on the triune soul leads Aelred to a knowledge of the triune God.[44]

Like the triune God of which it is an image, the soul exists in unity.[45] This is so because "the soul is a simple being, not made up of parts . . . ."[46] Reason, will, and memory are, then, merely three ways of expressing the powers that the soul exercises, the ways in which the soul functions. As Aelred puts it: "We refer to the soul as threefold because its powers are triple, *in* the memory, reason, and will."[47]

And so, for Aelred, the soul is an incorporeal, immortal, and conscious entity made in the image and likeness of God. Although the soul has components, these are merely convenient ways of expressing the soul's powers to remember, to think, and to choose. The soul is "one reasoning, willing, and remembering entity, to whose reason belongs consideration, to whose will choice, to whose memory remembering. So, by the reason the soul searches out or finds or considers God; by the will it chooses or neglects him, loves or despises him; by the memory it remembers, holds, and embraces him."[48] Through this statement, Aelred reveals the purpose of his detailed analysis of the soul: its faculties are the means by which it relates to God, who is the source of human happiness. The consequences of the soul's similarity to God are crucial to this quest for happiness:

> . . . The author of all natures has bestowed three [faculties] on this [human creature], which allow it to share in divine eternity, participate in divine wisdom, taste the divine delights. By these three I mean memory, knowledge [or understanding or reason], and love or will. Memory has the capacity for eternity, knowledge for wisdom, love for delight. In these three the human being was created in the image of the Trinity: memory held fast to God without forgetfulness; knowledge apprehended him without error; love embraced him without undue desire for any other thing. This was happiness.[49]

Happiness is the natural condition of humans—at least as intended by God.

1. The Intellect: Knowing the True and the Good

Although the physical powers of human bodies are no match for those of beasts,[50] humans possess in reason a power denied other animals:

So that you may know how little the body and sensation can do in comparison with reason, [I ask] what human could be secure from the hidden assaults of even one fly, if that fly were endowed, as is a human, with reason? If the fly wished otherwise, who could rest in peace or safely open his or her eyes? How many mortals could be murdered by one poisonous beast if, with the aid of reason, it could seek out their hiding place and [thus] plan the time, place, and means? How many cities and castles would be burned by sparrows and crows if reason prescribed a plan [showing them] what to do, where and when to do it, and what precautions to take? If the beasts and birds were equal to humans in reason, could they not make common cause and wipe out the whole human race?[51]

Humans do indeed possess an intellect, and this gives them an admirable advantage over animals who lack this gift.

Aelred's names for this faculty are many. He uses *animus* and *mens* for "mind."[52] Another term he uses is "reason" *(ratio)*.[53] And he is capable of combining *mens* and *ratio* into *mens rationalis,* a "rational mind."[54] In at least one case, Aelred uses *mens* and *intellectus* ("intellect" or "understanding") as equivalents.[55] Aelred seems much less concerned with terminological consistency than with the power of the intellectual faculty: "So great is the power of reason that by it we are distinguished from other animals and set above all of them."[56]

"The mind," Aelred says, "... is the head of the soul, where it is the seat of reason. From it are born the thoughts, as hairs from the head."[57] Thought is the activity of the intellect—an activity so important that Aelred repeats this message, again using the image of head and hair: "The hairs of our soul are subtle thoughts that proceed from the rational mind—which is, so to speak, the head of the soul."[58] Aelred thinks that reflection on one's own thought leads one to an awareness of the soul's existence and the rational faculty's function:

Now try, as much as you can, to put aside the bodily senses, concentrate, as much as you can, on the active power [of thought], and look closely at yourself thinking. Suppose you are in the dark, that you have closed your eyes and stopped up your ears, that your nostrils smell nothing and your palate tastes nothing, that you touch nothing. With all these [senses] at rest, now turn your attention to what it is that thinks so much, proposes and decides so much, turns over so many questions and makes such clear judgments on so many propositions. This is something great and sublime.[59]

Aelred concludes that it is the soul, through its rational faculty, that does this thinking.[60]

The rational soul does not simply think; it is capable of "recognizing the truth."[61] And because this is so, the intellect can provide necessary guidance in choosing the good: "What is done by the use of reason is rationally done; what is rationally done is rightly done; what is rightly done is well done."[62] Both truth and justice are thus accessible to humans through their power of reason, for "reason distinguishes between all these [data] and judges them, declaring one correct and another perverse, one just and the other unjust, one good and the other wretched."[63] Indeed, "to distinguish between what is just and what unjust is impossible without reason."[64]

The intellect's power, however, goes beyond the discernment of truth and justice. It has "a still higher power, and that is to see God."[65] Indeed, for Aelred, knowledge of truth and justice and knowledge of God are, on the highest level, the same knowledge.[66] To see truth, to see justice, to see God are all within the power of the intellect. But Aelred cautions his reader once more that the intellect is not a separate entity; rather, it is the rational power and discerning activity of the soul: "The word 'soul' signifies one thing to me, the word 'reason' another. But, concerning the one and same substance, which is the soul and reason, the word 'soul' expresses [the idea] that it lives, the word 'reason' that it discerns.... Nevertheless, there is one life of both, and there is one wisdom of both."[67]

2. The Will's Free Choice

"The will is itself nothing other than love," declares Aelred. "...The will of God is itself his love, which is nothing other than his Holy

Spirit, by whom love is poured out into our hearts [see Rom 5:5]."[68] Like the soul, of which it is a faculty or power, the will is an image of God, "so that it operates in the same way that the highest Goodness operates in all creation."[69] Thus, "according to its nature, the will is a great good and can never be anything but good."[70]

"... The power of the will is so great that, as far as I can see," says Aelred, "the whole worth of a person, good or bad, depends on it."[71] That power is the power of choice, which the will exercises in absolute freedom:

> So free is the rational will that it cannot be compelled to choose anything—not by humans, demons, angels, or any other creature. For God himself, from the moment at which he bestowed this freedom, has neither taken it away nor increased or diminished it. So the will cannot be forced, and nothing can be wrested from it. Apart from the will, all that a human being has lacks freedom.... The will alone is free, subject to no necessity.[72]

The only limitation on the will, Aelred thinks, is that it *must* choose—and constantly choose.[73]

But, in order to choose, one must know what one is choosing, and so the will requires the intellect's assistance: "Love [or will] always has reason [or intellect] as its companion, not that the will always loves [or chooses] reasonably, but so that it might discern, with alert circumspection, that which it chooses from those things which it rejects.... It is for love [or will], however, to choose what it wants for its use."[74] Thus, in Aelred's analysis, free choice is, in the end, dependent on the action of both the intellect and the will: "Because consent is made by the will and discernment by the reason, these two, will and reason, constitute free choice. The reason presents, so to speak, good or bad, justice or injustice, or things in between; the will consents, and whatever consent is made, is made only by the will."[75]

Aelred's presentation of this common action—and interaction—of the intellect and will is no mere intellectual exercise, because on it, he believes, human happiness depends, for choice or love of God and neighbor is the condition of happiness. The intellect takes the lead in this choice of the good: "Reason persuades us that we should love God because this is necessary and advantageous to us, because it is fitting that we do so. It is necessary so that we might avoid condemnation, advantageous so that we might obtain glorification, and fitting because God's loving us first makes him deserving of our loving him in return."[76] And, Aelred continues, "if the mind consents to this reasoning, it will be aroused to desire God by the will...."[77] But the intellect's work is not yet done; if human happiness is to result, the intellect must show the will the choices it must make to attain that object of its desire.[78]

The action to which the will is urged by the intellect can—and most often does—involve the activity of the body, which must be directed by the will.[79] Thus the will receives direction from the intellect; in turn the will directs the actions of the body. The result is the accomplishment of deeds that respond to God's precepts—all this necessary to human happiness. The will that chooses the good and directs human activities to its realization Aelred calls a just will.[80] As the body receives its perfection in immortality and beauty, as the intellect is perfected by knowledge, the perfection of the properly loving will is justice.

3. The Perceiving and Imagining Memory

The third power of the soul is memory, which is one with the other faculties in that it is a function of the soul, but differentiated in that it has a specific function "by which it remembers, by which it connects the sequence of preceding events, and those of the past and the future."[81] But recollection is not memory's only power; it also has powers of perception and imagination.

Perception is the process by which the soul becomes aware of the data provided by the body's senses. Through this power "the soul perceives colors, sounds, odors, tastes, and hardness and softness."[82] Through imagination the soul arranges the perceived data into a pattern comprehensible to the intellect.[83] Implicit in Aelred's description is an affirmation of the close association, the mutual dependence, the continuous interaction of soul and body.[84] Through its essential role as mediator, the memory is capable of a share in divine life. Aelred insists that "the memory has the capacity for God. From the moment that humans begin to know God, God begins to dwell in their memory, and they find him there as often as they think of him."[85]

4. The Affectus: *Attachment and Emotion*

To this point, Aelred's discussion of the soul clearly betrays the influence of Augustine of Hippo.[86] The triad of reason, will, and memory—and the image of the Trinity in that triad—constitute a recurring theme in Aelred's *On the Soul,* and are manifestly derived from Augustine's *On the Trinity.*[87] But Aelred offers an additional power or faculty of the soul: the *affectus.*

The word *"affectus"* admits no single definition or translation, but one of the ways in which Aelred uses the word conveys the meaning of "attachment."[88] Aelred explains this meaning of *affectus* in his *Mirror of Love:* "Attachment is a kind of spontaneous and delightful inclination of the spirit toward someone."[89] In one of Aelred's sermons, he gives a similar definition: "Attachment is, it seems to me, a sort of spontaneous inclination of the mind toward someone—an inclination accompanied by delight."[90] "Delightful" and "delight" are clearly words with an emotive content. And thus Aelred's soul is gifted with a faculty that goes beyond the traditional triad of intellect, will, and memory. To the rational, volitional, perceptive, and imaginative powers of these faculties Aelred adds the powers of emotion and feeling.

Human beings, Aelred firmly believes, are properly filled with emotions and attachments. To prove his point Aelred offers the example of Jesus of Nazareth, for "the God become man delighted in the human pleasure of attachment."[91] And Aelred excuses his emotions at the death of his friend Simon by pointing to the tears shed by Jesus at the death of his friend Lazarus.[92] Even unpleasant or aggressive feelings are not necessarily evil; Aelred can speak of being "besotted by anger,"[93] but he can also speak of "wholesome anger."[94] Both "good" feelings and "bad" feelings are natural and human, and thus can be morally good.

"Attachment," says Aelred, "is either spiritual, rational, irrational, dutiful, or natural—or, of course, physical."[95] He describes the origin of physical attachment in this way: "Frequently, it is not someone's virtue or vice but his or her outward appearance that attracts one's attention. An elegant exterior, a pleasant way of speaking, a proper bearing, a charming countenance easily invite and ensure attachment...."[96] Far from criticizing this very human sort of response, Aelred sees it as potentially productive of great good: "... Charm glowed in Moses," he writes, "so that, contrary to Pharaoh's decree,... he was kept unharmed by his parents for three months... 'because they had seen what an attractive infant he was [Heb 11:23; see Ex 2:2].' And when he was exposed to danger, his fine appearance attracted the affection even of Pharaoh's daughter [see Ex 2:3, 5]. She adopted him as her son [see Ex 2:10], and he then became great among all Pharaoh's servants."[97] Since Aelred believes the body to be good,[98] he sees no necessary evil in physical attraction and attachment.

Natural attachment is a still more obvious good for Aelred. It takes many happy forms: "There is the natural attachment everyone has for his own flesh, that of mother for her child, that of a person for his or her blood relatives."[99] Many of Aelred's examples are drawn from the Old Testament: the patriarchs' concern for the burial-place of their bodies, the solicitude, before Solomon, of the prostitute whose child was claimed by another, the fraternal attachment of Joseph, the mercy of David for his son Absolom.[100] The New Testament also provides Aelred models of natural attachment: "The Savior himself was filled with this wondrous compassion when he surveyed the city which was his according to the flesh and from which his forebears in the flesh had come. Moved by natural attachment, he wept profusely, pouring out tears for its [coming] destruction [see Lk 19:41]."[101] In addition to searching Scripture for examples of natural attachment, Aelred looks to its basis in the natural world: "The souls of animals are moved by... [natural] attachment, to the preserving, feeding, fostering, and protecting of their young, and also to the searching out of needed hiding-places, constructing nests, and cleverly preparing places suitable for their activities."[102] Natural attachments are good; birds and beasts share these with the Savior.

Natural attachment promotes the well-being of physical life, both human and animal. Dutiful attachment pertains to the right order of humans in society: "We call 'dutiful' that attachment which arises from agreeable service or compliance."[103] As social responsibility gives rise to attachment, so too does personal virtue. Virtue's attraction gives birth to an attachment Aelred calls "rational." "Rational attachment," he says, "arises from consideration of another's virtue: having discovered someone's virtue or holiness, either personally, by reputation, or, surely, through reading [about that person], our mind is flooded with a pleasant delight."[104]

The last of Aelred's attachments is spiritual attachment. "The spirit is stirred by this attachment," he tells us, "when, [touched] by a secret and apparently unforeseen visitation of the Holy Spirit, it is opened to the delights of divine love or to the pleasant nature of fraternal charity."[105]

There is surely an emotional content in all the attachments Aelred describes. But he also deals with the emotions more directly. Like perception and attachment, the emotions have their origin in the body or in physical occurrences and are felt in the soul. For example, Aelred writes of what he considers to be the proper response to the relics of the saints of Hexham: ". . . Our experience has verified the presence of these holy relics, which our faith has so long maintained; our sight has examined them, our hands have handled them, and our feelings *[affectus]* have tasted a draught of interior delight."[106] As the sensations provided by the body affect one's feelings, so too should the feelings be expressed exteriorly. Aelred tells his monks: "I want your face [to shine] with its former serenity, your mouth with affability, and your behavior with cheerfulness, so that, as the Holy Spirit nourishes you interiorly with grace, so your exterior should be attractively clothed."[107]

D. The Mutual Indwelling of Body and Soul

Thus the fulfillment, the happiness, of the whole person, which Aelred seeks, requires the interaction of body and soul. For its part, the soul gives life to the body: "In no way can the human body live

without the rational soul. So, from the time the body begins to live—
without any or [even] a momentary interval—it begins to have a
rational soul and to be a human, that is a rational, mortal animal."[108]
And, as the soul vivifies the body, it is active in the whole body "in
something of the same way that God acts in the universe."[109]

For its part, the body provides the soul the sense data without
which it cannot function: "Whatever is distinguished by the eyes,
whatever heard by the ears, whatever borne to the nostrils, whatever
touched by the hands, whatever tasted by the palate, is presented in
turn to the memory. On all of these reason passes judgment, and, on
the basis of this, the will makes its decisions."[110] The body also has
the task of carrying out these decisions. To will the good is insufficient; the body must do the good willed: "The testimony of a good
conscience [see 2 Cor 1:12] is born of two sources: from good works
and upright intention. For if one does not do the good, one cannot
have a good conscience. By the same token, if one does laudable
works and does not do them with an upright intention—but to gain
praise or some other temporal good—one cannot have a good conscience."[111] The body provides the raw material for the soul's perception, recollection, imagination, discernment, and decision; these
decisions are then carried out by the body.

The ideal human is, for Aelred, the natural human, natural in
that she or he has a body and a soul with natural powers that reflect
God's own powers. This ideal, natural human being is symbolized, as
Aelred sees it, by the prelapsarian Adam:

> Peace is yours, Adam, in eternity, in truth, and in love. Eter-
> nity gives peace to nature, truth to reason, love to the will.
> Peace existed in his [bodily] nature, which eternity saved
> from all corruption. Peace existed in his reason, which truth
> saved from all error. Peace existed in his will, which love
> saved from all selfish desire. From love came an upright will,
> from truth an enlightened reason, from eternity an incor-
> ruptible substance.[112]

It is difficult not to identify Adam's peace, reason, and love with the
happiness Aelred and all other humans so ardently desire to possess.

THE FUNCTIONS OF THE BODY AND SOUL

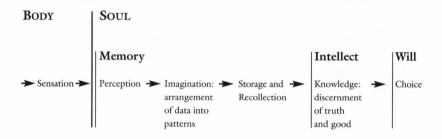

THE RELATIONSHIP BETWEEN BODY AND SOUL

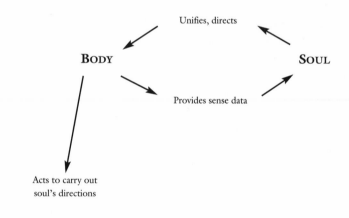

The condition of humans before the Fall is the state to which Aelred would return. He advises his monks—and everyone else who would listen—to

> consider the dignity of the first human condition, the dignity in which God created humans. You can see this dignity is

threefold: in liberty, in power, and in happiness. Adam was free, full of power, and happy. He had freedom in three ways: in his choice, his appetites, his activity. Before him stood good and bad, earth and heaven, death and life, happiness and wretchedness, the world and God. He had the freedom to choose among all these; he had freedom in his appetites. He did not selfishly desire the flesh rather than the spirit [see Gal 5:17]; he did not elect [to satisfy] any appetite he considered irrational. Rather, he chose what he wished, as much as he wished, and as he wished. He had freedom in activity, for he made use of this world to amass delights, to increase his happiness.... You may see his power from these words of God: "Increase and multiply, and fill the earth [see Gn 1:22]."[113]

"Thus," says Aelred, "his happiness was in the presence of God, the knowledge of God, the love of God. The presence of God was in his memory; his reason held his knowledge of God; his will embraced the love of God."[114] Adam symbolizes, for Aelred, the happy human —a human whose soul is united to God and whose body performs its absolutely necessary role in harmony with the soul.

III

Adam's Fall and Restoration

dam's bliss in Eden symbolizes, for Aelred, the happy human
being. Adam's body and his soul served him in harmonious
relationship. The mutually complementary faculties of Adam's
soul—intellect, will, memory, and *affectus*—provided him the means
to pursue a life of blissful freedom. But it is also in Adam that Aelred
sees the self-defeating choices that led to human misery. Adam
employs his precious gift of freedom to love, and thus to choose, a
life separated from his sole source of happiness, God. And thus, "by
withdrawing from God, he . . . delivers himself up to misery."[1] In
Adam, human beings, created in the image and likeness of God, have
chosen a self-centered love[2] and have plunged themselves into the
darkness of the land of unlikeness.[3]

The effects of this self-defeating choice are grave. Aelred asks himself: ". . . what has been destroyed in humans because of sin?"[4] His
response starts with those things not "destroyed." "Surely," he says, "not
the image [of God], which remains established in the essence and nature
of the rational human."[5] Aelred then addresses the effects of sin on the
soul's faculties: "Certainly memory remains in humans, though it is for-
eign to the recalling of God. The image remains in the reason, though it
is turned away from the light of the Creator's wisdom. The image per-
sists too in the will, though it is devoted to the self-centered desire for
imperfect things."[6] Thus, "though human nature has remained in its
integrity, . . . its likeness [to God] . . . has been lost through the failing of
the first parents. Splendor and beauty, so beneficial to humans themselves, have vanished. The ability to serve, potentially so profitable to
their neighbors, has likewise disappeared."[7] And then Aelred adds a most

devastating consequence: "There is no way humans themselves can restore these."[8] The human condition is not hopeless. But its restoration lies beyond human ability.

THE EFFECTS OF THE FALL

Faculty	Effect	And yet still
INTELLECT	Darkened	Can judge good and true from bad and false
WILL	Makes self-defeating choices; misdirects intellect, *affectus,* and body	Has free choice
MEMORY	Obscured, befuddled – recalls with difficulty – imagination concentrates on the harmful	Can remember —even God
AFFECTUS	Emotions and passions unrestrained	Remains good: attachments betrayed by the intellect; emotions and passions by the will
BODY	Senses dulled; subject to ills, suffering, and death	Remains good; not the flesh; impulses ill-regulated by the will, misdirected by the intellect, ill-served by memory

---

A. THE EFFECTS OF SIN ON THE SOUL

In an effort to explore further the consequences of Adam's sin, Aelred asks him: "How could you have contemplated such iniquity...?"[9] When Adam replies that he desired "...to be as a god [see Gn 3:5]," Aelred responds with indignation:

> What ingratitude! God created you in such a way that all creatures are either equal or inferior to you; only God is superior to you, and yet you envy him this superiority? I will be, he says, like a god! O intolerable pride! Only newly formed of earth and clay, do you insolently strive to become a god?...Thus pride paves the way for disobedience! These two sins, pride and disobedience, are the wretched condition and cause of all our sins.[10]

For Aelred, pride is the permeating vice of the intellect; pride is the ignorance in which one thinks oneself what one is not.[11] Disobedience is clearly a matter of the will's choice. Since the intellect presents the will with the information necessary to make its choices,[12] the prideful and hence ignorant intellect provides its false and misleading conclusions to a now perverse will, so that the will has an equally perverted basis for its disobedient and self-destructive choices.[13]

In the ignorance of pride, the intellect's judgment is painfully distorted: "Recall now," Aelred urges, "how the [first] humans have been depicted for you—how free, how powerful, how happy they were. And so too would have been their offspring—if their judgment had not been so radically injured."[14] This distorted judgment leads humans into folly: "In shedding, separating themselves from, the form [in which they had been created], miserable humans became like senseless beasts [see Ps 48:13] and began to be fools in fact and in deed...."[15]

The intellect, the eye of the soul, has indeed been darkened by sin. The effect of this darkening on the search for happiness is serious but not devastating.[16] Although the intellect may seem to be blinded by its own pride, the eye of the soul is not put out but, rather, stricken with a debilitating myopia. Aelred urges his audience to "see how humans exist in their misery and oppression. . . . They are infants and toddlers, who do not follow reason but only the desires of the flesh [see Gal 5:16]. . . . But, if they wish to grow to be young men and women, they must first take on themselves the yoke of fear of the Lord [see Lam 3:27]."[17] There is hope here. The human intellect can grow and leave behind its unreasoning infancy. The darkened vision of the soul can be corrected.

Although all humans, in the person of Adam, have freely chosen to reject their own happiness, they have not lost their power of free choice. That freedom can be directed still toward self-fulfillment or self-destruction: "Free choice . . . cannot be lost or diminished through sin or suffering. . . . So, whether you are able to accomplish the good by yourself or are less able and require the help of another, you always have free choice which you can use for the good, whether alone or with help. Hence it seems to me that sin is nothing else but free choice badly used, just as justice is nothing other than its good use."[18] But Aelred believes that, by and large, humans do use their free choice badly, thereby opting for self-destruction.[19] Thus it is precisely the power of free choice that is at the heart of human unhappiness, for it is possible to choose what one knows to be self-defeating.[20] The will is thus the primary source of human misery. The will can misdirect the intellect so that it does not see the truth, and even when the intellect is able to discern the good, the will can—and often does— direct the intellect's attention away from virtue, allowing the will to embrace vice.[21]

It is not that the will is by nature vicious; it is humans' perverse use of it that makes a "bad will."[22] Similarly, the free choice that humans possess is natural and thus good; its misuse is what is self-destructive.[23] The effects of sin are such that humans have a strong tendency—though not compulsion—to use free choice badly.[24]

Still, Aelred asserts, defects are not sins unless the will freely consents to them.[25] Temptations too are not in themselves sinful—unless the will chooses to accede to them. This Aelred shows through the life of Christ, who "himself suffered temptations," but remained without sin.[26] Nevertheless, if humans accede to temptation—as they sometimes do—this can lead to a self-defeating spiral downward into unhappiness;

then our will, "infected by the venom of self-centeredness and wretchedly trapped in the snare of sensual pleasure,...[is] by its own weight, born down ever lower from vice to vice...."[27] The result, for humans, of this descent is potentially catastrophic.[28]

Like the intellect and will, the memory has suffered from sin but has not been destroyed.[29] In a sense the memory works altogether too well, for it remembers not only God but also the illicit delights of the past.[30] Still, remembrance of evil is not the only difficulty that the fallen memory experiences. The imaginative powers of the memory are led by the misdirected choices of a fallen will to concentrate on those matters most harmful to the unhappy soul.[31] For Aelred, an imagination run riot is another part of the burden placed on the fallen human.

The *affectus* is also injured in the present human condition. Human emotions and attachments are, Aelred is convinced, clearly affected by the Fall. The betrayal of spiritual attachment Aelred illustrates with the example of King David's son Amnon, who "unhinged by attachment to culpable pleasure, was inflamed with an illicit desire to embrace his own sister.... No one should be disturbed at my calling this sort of attachment 'spiritual,' for it was born of spiritual villainy."[32]

Rational attachment, which arises from recognizing the virtue of another person,[33] can also be betrayed. Human judgment, impaired by a fallen intellect, can lead one to see vice for virtue, and thus move one to injurious attachment. And the fallen will is capable of overriding the intellect and choosing to attach itself to evil: "The opposite [of rational attachment] is the irrational, by which one is moved by an inclination of the mind toward someone—despite knowing of his or her vices."[34] But the betrayal of proper physical attachment is perhaps the most obvious of the effects of sin on the *affectus*. Aelred offers some Old Testament examples:

> No one of sound mind could doubt that one can be bedazzled by...the memory of harmful pleasure in all sorts of delights, and thus be moved to carnal attachment. At the sight of Bathsheba's beauty, this [sort of] attachment came unexpectedly upon David as he walked on the sun deck of his house [see 2 Sm 11:2]. It led him astray once he was

overcome and brought ruin on him once he strayed. It unnerved him in the unlawful embraces of another's wife, but it had the opposite effect in steeling him to the cruel destruction of his own soldiers [see 2 Sm 11:17]. This [same sort of] attachment blotted out [all] Solomon's wisdom, and, once he was led astray by carnal lust, it hurled him down into the chasm of spiritual fornication by his abominable worship of idols [see 1 K 11:1–8].[35]

All of these perversions of attachment clearly involve a misdirection of human passions and emotions.

Passions and emotions are often a source of confused agitation.[36] Humans, like the seas, are buffeted about by the ever-changing winds of those passions and emotions.[37] But despite the conflicting and seemingly contradictory demands made by the emotions, Aelred does not consider them evil. Human emotions, including the enjoyment of pleasure,[38] are good in themselves, but are squandered when "not ruled by reason."[39]

The *affectus* may be a continuous source of potentially devastating impulses to evil,[40] but it can also be a tool in pursuit of human happiness. Aelred describes the attachments and emotions as useful feet when directed by the will into the right path: "What are my feet but the attachments and emotions of the soul which the mind causes to proceed or give ground, judging [their path] as good or bad, desirable or repulsive, loving or hateful."[41]

B. THE BODY AND THE "FLESH"

The effects of the Fall on the body are obvious to Aelred: it is weak, subject to ills, suffering, and death.[42] The now necessary death of the body Aelred finds especially burdensome. Before the Fall, the first parents had, through God's gift, the possibility of immortality, a gift that they rejected.[43] The effects on their offspring are clear: "Since . . . we have all sinned in Adam [see Rom 5:12], so in Adam we have all heard: 'You are dust, and to dust you shall return [Gn 3:19].'"[44] But death is not the only burden of the postlapsarian body, for bodily

needs and impulses are "mixed with sin in us. Our hunger and thirst
are usually accompanied by evil self-centeredness, our sadness by
murmuring and despair or bitterness, our sleep by indifference to
restraint, and our weariness by tepidity and torpor."[45] The bodily
needs are not in themselves evil, but they are far too often associated
with vices that make those needs a burden to the spirit. However, the
needs of the human body are not the true source of the conflict
within humans—nor are the body's weakness and the strength of its
physical urges.

The real problem is not with the body but with the soul. To
Aelred, the body is not the "flesh" of which Paul spoke in Galatians
(5:17), describing the warfare between the flesh and the spirit.
Aelred reads Paul's "spirit"as a soul renewed by the infusion of God's
love. "By the word flesh," Aelred affirms, "Paul suggests the hapless
slavery of the soul caused by the remnants of our former [unre-
deemed] condition."[46] Thus Aelred sees the warfare within fallen
humans not as an opposition between body and soul, but as a conflict within the soul.

But the body is indeed ill-served by the postlapsarian soul. The
body's impulses are badly regulated by the intellect.[47] The memory
arouses these unregulated impulses through its recollection of past
passions and sins.[48] But it is the will that is the body's most treacher-
ous betrayer. The body's impulses toward sustenance, nurturing, and
procreation are all natural and good, but the human will abuses these
impulses by directing them to false ends.[49] Thus, it is an evil will that
is responsible for any transgressions committed by the body.[50] But,
given a good will, good works result, "works which we surely cannot
perform without our body."[51] Aelred likens the human body to "a
saucy serving girl,"[52] sometimes unruly but often mistreated by her
mistress, the soul. That mistress should use the body better by sup-
plying her physical needs,[53] regulating her unruly impulses,[54] and
directing her toward the good deeds she alone is capable of doing.

Despite the grim picture Aelred paints of the fallen condition of
humans, he admits that human life is a mixed bag that is not all bad.
Furthermore, he affirms the possibility that humans may, after all,
enjoy happiness. He tells us: "Too little is the good which humans

have in this life, because of the admixture of evil in it. They had a great deal of good in paradise, where there was no experience of evil. They shall have the perfect good in heaven, where no good they desire will be lacking, where no evil they fear will threaten them."[55] But, short of the complete happiness of heaven, is there no life on earth of which Aelred cannot say: "Many are the woes, many the miseries of this life"?[56]

C. THE GIFT OF HAPPINESS

Aelred maintains that human beings, are "created with a capacity for happiness,...[and] are eager for this happiness. But, by themselves, they are quite incapable of this happiness."[57] If human effort is insufficient in the most critical challenge facing them, their search for happiness, how is that happiness to be acquired? It is not acquired, Aelred asserts; it is received. The pilgrimage toward perfection, which is the glorious path that humans must take on the road to happiness, is accomplished in them, not by them. Aelred tells his monks: "...You, brothers, you are the tabernacle of God; you are the temple of God. As the apostle says: 'The temple of this God is holy, and this [temple] you are [1 Cor 3:17].' A temple, because the Lord will reign forever in you. Yet still a tabernacle, for he travels about in you, hungers in you, thirsts in you."[58] The spiritual life, then, is a pilgrimage in which God moves those on the path. It is a gift, and the God who gives this gift is an "ever gentle, tender, loving and compassionate" God.[59] For Aelred, the initiative lies always—from beginning to end—with God. The beginning of the spiritual life, which he describes through the use of the word "conversion," is not an act of the sinner but a gift of a loving and compassionate God.[60] And, at each stage of the human pilgrimage toward happiness, God provides the gifts that effect the restoration of Adam's children.[61] For Aelred, these gifts are all contingent on the one great gift of God: the overwhelmingly generous gift of himself in the incarnation of the Second Person of the Trinity.[62] As Aelred says, "without Christ we can do nothing."[63]

THE ACTION OF GRACE AND FREE CHOICE
IN ACCOMPLISHING THE GOOD

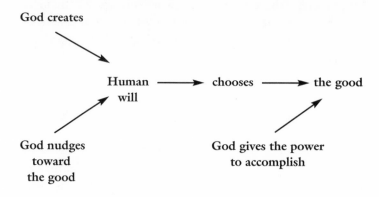

And he adds: "What does anyone have which he or she has not received [see 1 Cor 4:7]? But if humans have received grace, why should they be praised as if they merited it? To you, then, my God, belong praise, glory, and thanksgiving; to me, however, belongs only embarrassment because all that is evil in me I have done, and all the good in me I have received."[64] For Aelred this is not a cry of despair but another affirmation of the goodness of God toward one incapable of attaining the good that will bring him happiness. For Aelred, everything good in human life is God's gift, and he affirms that "all this [good] flows forth from the font of his loving kindness; all emanates from his affectionate heart."[65]

But if all that is good in humans is gift, as Aelred asserts, how can he also affirm, as he does, that free choice remains a human power even after the Fall?[66] Sometimes Aelred attempts to clarify the issues involved in this knotty problem in ways that seem either inconsistent or inadequate.[67] At times he seems to suggest that God bestows grace on humans in response to their good works—works that imply a free choice. He writes, for example: "It is clear that everywhere 'is the power of God and compassion,... for you [God] will give to every person according to his or her works [Ps 61:12–13].'"[68] This passage is from a sermon on the burdens of Isaiah, and it is understandable that the exhortation to virtue common to many sermons should sound semi-pelagian, should seem to make the conferral of grace contingent on human choice. But Aelred emphatically rejects this position, with an economy of language unusual for him: "He [the Holy Spirit] conferred justice on humans; he did not give back justice as a reward."[69] Indeed, he says, properly disposed persons "recognize that whatever good is in them is his [God's] gift."[70]

Aelred goes further. It is by God's gift alone that humans exercise their free choice in opting for the good: "In order that the work God accomplishes in us might be ours, he inclines our will so that we might consent to it. Thus, thanks to his grace, the reward becomes ours. If I do the work willingly, I also receive the reward. But, so that I might be willing to do the good work, it is God who causes even my willing [see Rom 9:16]."[71] God's grace initiates the process of choice by nudging the will toward the good. Thus grace must come to the will even before its choice, and without this prevenient grace no choice could be good. Aelred writes: "Even the unjust have free choice, for without it they could not even be unjust. . . . No one can be either just or unjust except through the will and, hence, through free choice. But grace alone arouses the will to justice; in injustice the will hurls itself down."[72]

The human will is thus the recipient of a freely given impetus that inclines it toward the good. And Aelred sees God giving this prevenient grace to many whose past lives show no inclination toward the good. Aelred offers the examples of Jesus' loving treatment of the adulterous woman in John 8:3–11 and of the paralyzed man in Mark 2:3–12. Aelred's exegesis of the story of the adulteress gives no indication that Jesus' loving kindness was bestowed on her because of her prior repentance. Moreover, Aelred seems to make the woman's adultery the occasion for her forgiveness: "Happy was the woman, I would say, in this adultery, absolved from her past and freed from care for her future."[73]

The forgiveness and healing of the paralytic offers Aelred the occasion for a more explicit commentary on prevenient grace: "That happy man received forgiveness for his sins, without asking, without any prior confession, without any deserving reparation, without any

evocative contrition. It was bodily health for which he asked, not
that of the soul; yet he received health of both body and soul."[74] For
Aelred, God's gifts precede any human response, but that precedence
does not destroy free choice in humans. He writes:

> The [prevenient] grace of God operates so that they might
> will the good, not by destroying free choice—without which
> they could not will anything at all—but by influencing them
> to will the good. Consequently, when you do something
> good, do not think you do this good through your own
> power. Nevertheless, do not think the deed independent of
> your will, since a work cannot be called good unless it is also
> voluntary.[75]

Thus, for Aelred, God begins the process of human salvation, but
humans have the freedom—and the need—to respond to prevenient
grace.

The work of human salvation is, from start to finish, God's work,
but human choice continues to be necessary to effect the good chosen. The human who does not reject prevenient grace and chooses the
good must still accomplish—and continue to will to accomplish—that
good. But once more, it is God who effects, by his grace, the good
desired by humans. Aelred writes: "It seems to me that, when it
[Scripture] speaks [in Gal 5:16] of 'walking in the spirit,' we may
understand this not as our spirit but as the Holy Spirit, who accomplishes in us the good desired."[76] Aelred amplifies:

> ... That [desire] of the spirit which we quite properly call love
> [is] surely not our spirit but the Spirit of God, for "the love of
> God has been poured out into our hearts by the Holy Spirit,
> who has been given to us [Rom 5:5]." Between these two
> [our spirit and the Holy Spirit], I say, there is that in humans
> which is called free choice, somehow occupying a middle
> place, so that, to whichever of these two the soul turns, it
> doubtless acts by free choice. No one would be so foolish as to
> dare to ascribe to humans, on the basis of free choice, an equal
> aptitude for good and bad. This because "we are not sufficient

to claim anything as coming from ourselves [2 Cor 3:5]," since "it is God who works in us, both to will and to accomplish, according to his good will [Phil 2:13]." All this "depends on God's showing mercy [Rom 9:16]."[77]

But, Aelred quickly adds, "Do all these texts deny that free choice exists in humans? Far from it!"[78]

For Aelred, the human will does indeed choose freely, even though God, through a gift or grace, inclines the will toward the good and then, also as a gift, bestows on human beings the power to effect that good. Aelred asks again: "Is it so that he [God] takes away free choice from you, destroys your will, and withdraws the judgment of reason?" Again Aelred answers: "Far from it!"[79] He then explains that the human role lies "in acting in consent to his [God's] action and thus cooperating with him. If he should act by me or through me, but against my will, I should not be able to exclaim [with Paul in 2 Tm 4:7]: 'I have fought the good fight; I have finished the course; I have kept the faith.'"[80]

But, Aelred insists, free choice "does not suffice for any good, but in it or with it or through it God accomplishes many good works. In it, when, by a hidden inspiration, he arouses [our choice] for some good. With it, when he joins the consent of our free choice to his purpose. Through it, when, by God's cooperation, the one [free choice] accomplishes [good] through the other [God's grace]."[81] And thus Aelred can conclude that the "merit is ours; the grace is God's. For these merits he gives life eternal, grace for grace. He returns to each according to his or her works [see Mt 16:27; Rom 2:6]. But all these works receive their reward because he bestows first, and bountifully, his gifts. That eternal life is a grace, listen to him [to Paul] once again: 'For the wages of sin are death, but the grace of God is eternal [Rom 6:23].'"[82]

As Aelred sees the process of human perfection and salvation, then, God first nudges the will toward the good (prevenient grace). Then, if the human will chooses the good, God provides—again as a gift or grace—the power to accomplish the good. God attributes merit to the person in whom the good is thus accomplished, and he gives the gift of salvation to that person. All of this presupposes, of course, that human beings have received their very existence—and, thus, their will—as a gift of God.[83] The grace is fourfold; yet the happiness of humans is accomplished without violating their freedom of choice.

Aelred sees humans—himself included—as rewarded with happiness because of the good works they do, but, he asserts, "that I may be willing to do a good work, it is God who works in my willing [Rom 9:16]. Then, having aroused that will to seek, to ask, to knock, he gives grace upon grace to complete what the good will chooses."[84] The result is a life filled with those things that Aelred treasures as most precious:

> Wherever there is peace, wherever tranquility, wherever heavenly serenity smiles, wherever there is leisure for knowing, for wisdom, or for contemplation, in all these "taste and see how sweet is the Lord [Ps 33:9]." But where in this is our own virtue and industry? Rather, it is the voice of the Spirit who, speaking and working within, "provides for the deer and discloses that which is dense, so that in his temple all speak of his glory [Ps 28:9]."[85]

IV
Humility:
The Perfection of the Intellect

To be fully human—and, thus, to be happy—the children of Adam must exercise all their faculties to the fullest; they must use their God-given and God-restored powers of body and soul. For Aelred, the faculty of the soul that most clearly identifies the human being as human is the intellect.[1] To be fully human, "to be a human of 'the finest gold [Is 13:12],' one must live according to reason, not according to the senses in the manner of beasts."[2]

But the human intellect has been darkened as a result of the Fall,[3] and humans are unhappy.[4] This unhappiness is due, in large part, to their ignorance of what happiness is: "Although they long ardently for happiness, not only do they not do those things by which they might attain their goal, they rather direct their affection to lesser things and do that which will add still more to their misery. In my view, they would not do this if a false image of felicity did not delude them . . . ."[5] Because of this delusion, humans seek happiness where it cannot be found. And thus unhappiness is, in large part, the consequence of the intellect's ignorance of the true source of happiness.[6]

A. Pride: The Enemy of the Intellect

The nature of happiness, of fulfillment, is clearly contingent on the nature of the being to be fulfilled, of the sort of being that is searching for happiness. Ignorance of what one is—and, thus, of what will bring

41

one fulfillment—is, therefore, the root cause of human misery. If one tries to be what one is not, one will necessarily be frustrated in the attempt and make oneself miserable. Aelred is sure that this is what happened in the primordial Fall; for it was the leaven of pride that "puffed up the [first] man, so that he wished to be as a god [see Gn 3:5]."[7] The pride of seeing oneself as something other than what one is constitutes for Aelred the heart of Adam and Eve's self-destructive sin. Adam's pride and Eve's lack of understanding provided

> the right moment for the ancient serpent. "Why," he asked, "has the Lord commanded you not to eat of this tree [see Gn 3:1]?" "Taste it, and you will be as gods [Gn 3:5]." At these words the woman's heart swelled up. This is surely pride! How much, do you think, did she delight in hearing that through pleasure one can reach out to divinity? How could it be otherwise? What has been offered is sweet; what has been promised is glorious. She tasted, and everything broke with a crash. For what followed was not glory but ignominy, not divinity but unhappiness, not exultation but confusion.[8]

Aelred sees this prideful fall of the first parents as a loss to all of humankind. "Why," he asks, "did we lose the glory in which we were created? Why were we driven out into this misery? What is the cause of all this, brothers, except pride?"[9]

Self-deceptive pride takes many forms, Aelred insists, against all of which humans must fight:

> We see pride under the forms of vanity, ambition, boasting, contempt of God, and self-love. Vanity is in action when we delight in the praise of others. Ambition is present when we set ourselves up to take charge of others. Boasting is apparent when we wildly claim that whatever good there might be has been produced by us. Contempt is seen when we believe others are pitiful. Self-love occurs when we spurn the judgment of others and delight in our own supposed virtues and not in those of God.[10]

It is to the last of these that Aelred devotes much of his attention. Self-love is for him a particularly vicious form of pride, for it falsely attributes to humans what belongs to God: virtue and goodness.

In all the practices of the spiritual life, Aelred thinks, there is danger of self-congratulation: "If we should make progress in knowing God, if we should penetrate Scripture's hidden meaning a bit more subtly, if we should overflow with tears, if we should be solemn in our speaking and mature in our manner, and, as a result of all these, we should become proud, then it would not be said of us: 'She will return to him good, not evil [Prv 31:12].'"[11] And, Aelred is sure, all virtues practiced and good deeds done are wasteful and destructive to one who does them out of pride.[12] It is precisely those "placed on the heights of virtue" who must beware of "beginning to glory in themselves and not in God [see 1 Cor 1:31]."[13] The battle against pride is thus a life-long struggle, especially for those who most avidly pursue perfection.[14]

B. THE RESTORATION OF TRUE VISION

The healing and restoration of the human intellect requires, of course, the action of God.[15] The result of that grace-full action, the recognition of one's own frailty, is a central component of the restoration of truth to the intellect. For it is through humility that humans know themselves as they truly are.[16] Aelred's humility is not meekness; it has nothing to do with the conventional picture of the humble person sitting piously with downcast eyes. Aelred's humility is a lifting up of the intellect's eyes to see the truth about oneself, for "those who have humility look at themselves properly...."[17] For Aelred, the most important element in self-knowledge is the recognition that one's virtues are not one's own.[18] The proper response "of the humble is to glory not in themselves but in the Lord."[19]

Aelred urges his readers to imitate the Christ whom he sees as both source and exemplar of humility. It is the birth of Jesus that provides Aelred with a most convincing example of humility:

So that humans might eat the bread of angels, you [Jesus] took on yourself the husk of our poverty, the ashes of our mortality, the leaven of our infirmity. Thus the bread of angels became a man; he who is great was made a small child; he who is rich became a poor infant. All this so that you [humans] who are great in your own eyes might be made little children through humility, you who are rich in self-centeredness might become poor infants through the rejection of your wealth. Thus, when you are born spiritually, you [too] might not find room in the inn [see Lk 2:7]. Then you would no longer rely on your own will, your own capacities, your own knowledge, your own industry, but on the judgment of another. Then you would eat your bread with ashes when the Lord feeds you with the bread of tears and gives you abundant tears as your drink [see Ps 79:6]. Thus would you be born in Christ and Christ in you.[20]

The Incarnation, the greatest of God's many graces,[21] provides a model for the human response to that grace.

Christ's mother Mary provides Aelred with another model of humility. Aelred counsels his readers to turn their

thoughts for a moment to the perfection which shone bright in the blessed Mary. She never became proud over the grace conferred on her, as is shown by her humble response to the angel: "Behold the handmaiden of the Lord [Lk 1:38]." That she did not think herself superior to others because of it is shown by that humble visitation which she, who carried God in her womb, undertook in order to bring greetings to [another] handmaid [her cousin Elizabeth; see Lk 1:39–40].[22]

Aelred urges his audience: "You ought first to meditate on that wondrous humility of our Lady, and then imitate her as much as possible."[23]

In humility the intellect's likeness to God will be restored. Aelred tells his readers that "it is obvious . . . that pride has led humans away from the highest good, not by the stride of the foot but by an attachment of the mind. It has made them decrepit and has disfigured God's likeness in them. Just so, by humility, which draws one near to God through the mind's attachment, humans are restored to the likeness of him who created them."[24] This restoration of the intellect will begin to bring the happiness rational humans know to be their goal.

C. MEDITATION: THE PATH TO HUMILITY

Humility, true knowledge of oneself, is a virtue difficult to attain, a virtue that requires great effort. The means offered by Aelred is meditation, at one and the same time a laborious task and an easy burden.[25] Meditation involves intense intellectual activity. In his treatise *On Reclusion,* for example, when Aelred urges the recluse "not to omit the gifts of the Magi in her meditation,"[26] she is to "study this diligently with her mind," as she did in considering the shepherds' vigil.[27] When meditating on "the pleasures of heaven and the delights of Paradise," she is to "reflect on all these things in her mind . . . ."[28] Similarly, in a sermon on the Ascension, Aelred advises that in meditation "we ought to ponder with a diligent mind . . . ."[29] So pervasive is Aelred's insistence on this intellectual effort that, in Book 2 of his *Mirror of Love* alone, he makes twenty references[30] to the insight obtained by mental examination, perception, watching, taking heed, recognition, and imagination.[31]

The last, imagination, is a function of the memory, as Aelred sees it,[32] and thus meditation, though primarily an activity of the intellect, requires the use of other human faculties as well. Perhaps better put, Aelred sees meditation as the activity of the whole person, of the person's intellect, will, memory, and *affectus* together. In meditation Aelred sees his readers using their intellects to see, their wills to love, their memories to imagine, and their *affectus* to embrace[33] the objects of their meditation.

All this requires time, which must be set aside for the purpose of meditation.[34] Aelred finds early morning an especially opportune time for meditation; in *On Reclusion* he advises the recluse that "when the holy vigils are ended, she should spend the interval between the night's [office of] lauds and morning in prayer and meditation...."[35] I suspect Aelred's enthusiasm for this early hour stems from the stillness associated with that time of day, for he insists that meditation requires a quiet environment.[36] To meditate "one [must] withdraw from the uproar outside into the secret retreat of one's own mind and, once the gate is closed on the surrounding throng of noisy trifles, survey one's interior treasures...."[37]

Once a person has taken the time necessary to meditate and has arranged a suitably quiet environment in which to meditate, Aelred is sure that the happy toil involved in meditation will have a salutary effect. Properly pursued, meditation's effect is the humility of self-knowledge, the fundamental goal of the exercise: "...Those who apply their mind diligently to the face of their soul, as if in a mirror, will find, if I am not mistaken, not only whatever deformity they have in them, but, in the light of truth, they will also recognize the hidden causes for this deformity. And so they will blame them not on the harshness of the Lord's yoke, which is not harsh at all, but on their own perversity."[38]

But self-knowledge is not the only intellectual consequence of meditation. Some knowledge of God may also be gained in meditation.[39] The ordering of God's world is also open, at least in part, to the intellect of the one who meditates:

If you desire to have revealed to you the knowledge of hidden matters or the solution to some questions, if you wonder uneasily at the causes and reasons for the confusion in the world, if you are disquieted because you see the peace enjoyed by sinners who take no part in human toil and are not scourged like other humans [see Ps 72:5], then seek a retreat where you may converse with Jesus, one on one. ...He will come in the form of a most agreeable teacher, bearing in his right hand the law all aflame, to illuminate you with knowledge of the law and to set you afire with the love which comes from meditation on the law.[40]

Aelred's optimistic assessment of the fruits of human effort in meditation are here present, complemented by his insistence that the
knowledge acquired is a gift. Those who habitually turn their gaze
inward in meditation will eventually discover in themselves

> nothing disturbing or disordered, nothing to torment or
> worry them, but, rather, everything delightful, everything
> harmonious, everything peaceful, everything tranquil. The
> entire throng of their thoughts, words, and deeds will be like
> the best ordered and most peaceful family; on this household
> they will smile in their souls like the father of the family. This
> will immediately give rise to a marvelous security, from that a
> marvelous joy, and from that a sort of jubilation which will
> burst forth still more devoutly in praise of God the more
> clearly they see that whatever good there is in them is his
> gift.[41]

Meditation thus leads to a humility that contributes mightily to human
happiness.

1. Meditation on and Through Nature

Aelred's biographer, Walter Daniel, writes of Aelred's meditative
approach to nature: "Whenever he pondered the beauty, arrange-
ment, or worth of the created [world], he saw in the transitory him
who is not able to pass away, 'with whom there is no change or
shadow of alteration [Jas 1:17].' In meditating on the harmony
among the variety of essences and substances in the created universe,
he realized how wonderful must be he who created all these."[42]
Apparently Walter's assessment is correct, for Aelred's enthusiasm for
the beauties of nature is matched only by his certainty that meditation on nature leads to knowledge of God: "There is apparent in
nature an immensity in which divine power is seen to be impressed as
a sort of footprint. Beauty, which is discerned in some way in the
form and appearance of all creatures, is properly imputed to [God's]
wisdom. Again, the [obvious] utility of things is properly assigned to

divine goodness."[43] God's power, wisdom, and goodness are thus all apparent in his creatures, in nature.

Still more fundamentally, Aelred sees all creatures infused with God's love—and thus worthy of meditative contemplation: "If you closely contemplate every creature, from first to last, from highest to lowest, from the loftiest angel to the lowliest worm, you will surely discover divine goodness—which we call by no other name than his love. This love contains all, embraces all, and penetrates all . . . ."[44]

2. Meditation on and Through Scripture

Aelred's enthusiasm for Scripture as a source for meditation he makes clear everywhere in his works. A short but effective statement of that enthusiasm occurs in one of his sermons for All Saints day: "See in holy Scripture how great are its depths, how its mysteries overflow the heavens."[45] Aelred is sure "the teachings of Jesus . . . are contained in the holy Writ, which the Spirit dictated . . . ."[46] The truth of Scripture, therefore, stems from its ultimate, infallible source. Thus, those who meditate on Scripture are guided to that truth: "The star, brothers, which guides us to Jesus is holy Scripture."[47]

The effects of scriptural meditation are so beneficial that Aelred is compelled to make the considerable effort required. The time needed—and the withdrawal from everyday concerns demanded—are small prices to pay when he considers the reward: ". . . If we wish to see with the eyes of our spirit Jesus' ascent to heaven, and if we wish to reach heaven with and through him, we must go forth from the world by reflection and contemplation."[48] Scripture is a sure guide to the reflections of those seeking perfection and to their efforts in that pursuit: "It is necessary that we subject all our plans, all our thoughts, meditations, behavior, and decisions to scrutiny in the light of holy Scripture . . . ."[49] When the path to perfection is not clearly discerned, Scripture dispels the darkness.[50] Scripture also provides both clarity and consolation in the human struggle, for "however much exterior persecution may sadden us, so much does the consolation of holy Writ gladden us."[51] For Aelred, then, Scripture is, as he says, "the font of all learning."[52] And, in learning from Scripture, the person pursuing instruction is following the example of Jesus himself: "In this dutiful conduct [the worship of God], we are instructed by the search into holy Scripture, to which the twelve-year-old Jesus encourages us by his example of sitting in the temple, in the midst of the elders, listening to them and asking them questions [see Lk 2:46]."[53]

Aelred offers many examples of a meditative approach to the Scriptures. He begins one of these, his treatise *On Jesus at the Age of Twelve,* with this response to the request of his friend Ivo: "You ask of me, my dear son Ivo, that I might draw out some seeds for devout meditation and holy love from that passage of the gospel reading which tells of the good deeds of the twelve-year-old boy Jesus. You ask that I might commit them to writing and send you what I have gathered in my little baskets."[54] Aelred offers his response in three "little baskets," the first of which contains a commentary on the historical, or literal, meaning of the passage in Luke (2:42–50) that tells the story of the boy Jesus' sojourn in the temple. Aelred begins with an imaginative recreation of the subject of his reflection:

> . . . You [Ivo] begged me to reveal to you where the boy Jesus was during those three days when his mother was searching for him, where he found lodging, what food he ate, in what company he took delight, what matters occupied him. I sense, my son, I sense that, in your holy prayers, you often ask these questions of Jesus himself, with familiarity, affection, and tears. You ask when you have before your heart's eyes the delightful image of that dear boy, when you depict, with your spiritual imagination, the features of his handsome face, when you plainly perceive his eyes, at once charming and gentle, radiating their joyful beams upon you.[55]

After inquiring of Jesus about his activities during the three days, Aelred turns to questions of deeper spiritual significance: he asks Jesus about his apparent lack of compassion for his searching mother, and he asks Mary about her sorrow in that search.[56] Aelred extends his search for the what and why of this three-day event in a meditation that takes up some seven more pages in the critical edition.[57]

But Aelred offers still more. His second "little basket" is filled with the results of his reflection on the allegorical significance of Jesus' youthful sojourn in Jerusalem. One example may suffice:

> "The boy Jesus stayed on in Jerusalem, and his parents did not know this [Lk 2:43]." Christ is still in the Church, and the Jews, his parents according to the flesh, do not know it. [This] Joseph is still in Egypt, and it is in the Egyptian language, not in Hebrew, that he is styled "savior of the world" [see Gn 41:45]. While he distributes the corn of his wisdom to the Egyptians—that is, to the gentiles—his brothers waste away with hunger among the Canaanites—that is, among unclean spirits.[58]

Aelred's third "little basket" contains the "moral sense"[59] of the short passage in Luke describing the stay of the boy Jesus at the temple. Here Aelred sees in each year of Jesus' life a spiritual activity, gift, or virtue.[60] Here too, in Jesus' journeys from Bethlehem to Nazareth to Jerusalem, Aelred discerns the progress toward perfection of those seeking true happiness.[61] Aelred concludes this section, and his treatise, with the words:

> Behold, my dear friend, that for which you have asked. Though it responds only inadequately to your desire, your attachment, your expectation, yet it is, if I am not mistaken, some indication of my intentions and of some sort of effort. And know that I have not tried to expound on this lesson from the gospel, but to elicit from it, as you asked, some seeds for your meditation.[62]

Aelred's meditative technique is a threefold approach to Scripture, requiring an imaginative construction of the context of the biblical passage, intense effort to draw forth the spiritual implications of the passage thus set in context, and an internal response in the form of resolutions or prayers. In this way Aelred hopes to experience the "spiritual taste"[63] of the text on which he meditates.

Aelred's model of the virtuous meditator is Mary, the mother of Jesus. In his *On Jesus at the Age of Twelve*, he asks:

> What is the meaning of the evangelist's report: "They did not understand the word he had said to them [Lk 2:50]"? I do not think this was said of Mary. From the moment the Holy Spirit came over her and the power of the most High overshadowed her [see Lk 1:35], she could not be ignorant of her son's plan. But, while the others did not understand what he had said, Mary "kept all these words in her heart [Lk 2:51]," so that she might know and understand. She kept them in her memory, she ruminated on them in her meditations, and she connected them with the other things she had seen and heard of him.[64]

The subject of Mary's meditations was the "word," the sayings and doings of Jesus; she held them in her memory, and she "ruminated" on them. It seems that here Aelred is illustrating through Mary the meditative practice through which twelfth-century monks, Aelred included, attempted to respond to their *Rule*'s injunction to engage in "spiritual reading."[65] Aelred's word here for the process of meditation is *ruminabat*, "ruminated," or "chewed the cud." Scripture provides the grass, the memory holds the cud thus produced, and in meditation Mary chews the cud, providing nourishment for her soul.

Aelred's "reading" of Scripture is a slow, meditative process. In the course of his lengthy meditation on the life of Christ in *On Reclusion*, Aelred frequently urges his reader to maintain a measured pace. For example, after his meditation on Christ's washing of his disciples' feet, he says to the viewer of this scene: "Why do you hurry to leave? Hold yourself back a little while."[66]

But all this intense, though measured, activity will not avail to make meditation efficacious unless it is a response to God's initiative. Only his gifts, his grace, will make Scripture come alive in the mind of the meditator.[67] Given God's grace and human effort, the wisdom apparently hidden in Scripture can be attained: "Holy Scripture can be understood through the belly [see Is 16:11] of God, in which

Scripture's secrets are contained, as if in the belly's inner parts. There his various judgments and precepts, joined into one faith by rational consideration, send forth a most pleasant melody to the hearts and ears of the faithful."[68]

3. Meditation on Oneself

One meditates on nature and Scripture to attain knowledge, which Aelred knows fills and fulfills the human intellect. Since a principal goal of meditation is to achieve at least a measure of self-knowledge, or humility, it is not surprising that Aelred urges his readers to meditate on themselves. In one of his Lenten sermons he says: "We must first consider where we have been, where we are, for what we must hope, and what we must fear."[69] This consideration of "where we are" is, of course, not spatial but moral: "Let each and every one now consider themselves; let them see how they stand before the Lord [by asking] how they have lived in his sight."[70]

Aelred also advises that meditation on self include a temporal dimension. Our past is a fruitful source of meditation, even though its results may be painful when we recollect "those faults we have committed and those delusions we have pursued."[71] But the remembrance of past sin has a salutary effect on earnest pursuers of perfection.[72] Aelred also urges meditation on one's present status. Here is such an admonition in a passage broadly satirical:

Placing before yourself these attestations of the evangelical and apostolic teaching . . . as before a spiritual mirror, contemplate carefully your soul's countenance. If you find yourself floating to feasts, frequently glowing from wine unmixed with water, entangled in secular affairs, filled to the brim with worldly cares; if you find yourself brooding over fleshly desires, occupied all day with quarrels and gossiping, tearing your sisters' and your brothers' flesh to pieces with shameful disparagement; if you find yourself sitting sluggishly in dissolute inactivity, reacting restlessly to all sorts of stimuli, flitting excitedly hither and yon; if you find yourself zealously procuring delicacies for your belly, not by your own toil but by the blood and sweat of the poor; if you find yourself besotted by anger, impatience, envy, and disobedience, taking greater care of your belly than of your mind; if you ceaselessly transgress the limits of your profession; if you strut around sleek and fat in the midst of all this, do not, I beg you, do not boast much about your paltry tears....[73]

One can easily imagine Aelred's audience responding to this with intense amusement, but also catching some glimpse of themselves in the mirror he holds out for their meditation. Aelred surely believes that, if one reacts properly to one's present state, this can lead to fruitful resolutions for the future.[74] Aelred also urges careful meditation on that future—a future that will inevitably bring one's death: "Solomon testifies to the usefulness of meditation on death when he says: 'Son, always keep in mind your last day, and you will never sin [Si 7:40].' Do those who delight in sinning keep their end before their eyes? Cry out, then, O sinner, in repentance, lest you be driven out in punishment. Let the thought of the day of the Lord sour you to worldly pleasures, lest you then experience great bitterness...."[75]

Aelred matches this warning about the future with great confidence in the ability of his audience to respond to God's call to reject pride and don the mantle of humility. Aelred's confidence is based on his solid conviction that all humans are immersed in an ocean of God's love. He urges everyone to "see how we are surrounded by love....With true humility reigning in our heart, we are ever aroused to remembrance of our sins and are likewise called forth by continual and accurate consideration of the good we do."[76] Aelred thus sees humility as a self-knowledge that demands acknowledgment both of human weakness and of human glory. And that glory he knows comes from the great worth of humans as redeemed by Christ.[77] Aelred sees humans as people purchased at great price; he hopes that, by meditation, those people thus redeemed will recognize their true condition.

4. Meditation on God

Aelred urges all those who seek happiness in perfection to "delight greatly in the contemplation of God...."[78] Aelred offers an example of meditation on God's overwhelming attributes when considering the three days that the boy Jesus spent in the temple:

> The first day on which the soul thirsting for God tarries in the delights of observation, as if in Jerusalem, is the contemplation of divine power. The second day is astonishment at God's wisdom. The third is the foretaste of his goodness and gentle kindness. To the first truly belongs justice, to the second knowledge, to the third loving-kindness. . . . On the first day, that fear which follows from the consideration of justice purifies the soul. Thus purified, wisdom enlightens it. Thus enlightened, goodness rewards it with an infusion of delight. You see, I am sure, how necessary and useful it is, amid the activity of good deeds, to spend these three days in the delights of Jerusalem . . . .[79]

Those who meditate on God's admirable attributes will gain insights of a profound nature: "In God's power [they will see] the depths of his judgments; in his wisdom, his hidden purposes; in his goodness, the unutterable words of his loving-kindness."[80] But it is the awesome transcendence of God,[81] expressed through these attributes, that leads Aelred to approach God through meditation on the Incarnate Word of God. And so, most of Aelred's meditations are directed toward Jesus, whose life, death, and resurrection, Aelred thinks, reveal God to an extent that would not otherwise be possible. The resurrection, for example, provides humans an access to the invisible things of God, as it did for Jesus' disciples:

> It was necessary, brothers, that his disciples, who to this point [in Jesus' ministry] had been but children, be fed with this milk [of his resurrection]. They were such children that they had fled from him, had deserted him in his suffering [see Mt 26:56]. Peter was such a child that he denied Jesus because of the challenge of a single serving-girl [see Mt 26:69–74]. So it was necessary for them, who were like children, to see, with their physical eyes, his resurrection, and

thus be fed as if with milk, so that they might be capable of believing what they could not see, of contemplating the invisible.[82]

Aelred takes Christ's humanity, and thus his accessibility, very seriously. In his reconstruction of the agony of Christ in the garden of Gethsemane, Aelred addresses the prostrate Jesus: "You have such compassion for me that you show yourself so human that you seem not to know that you are God. You pray prostrate on your face, and 'your sweat has become like drops of blood trickling down to the ground [Lk 22:44].'"[83]

For those pursuing knowledge of God—and thus deeper knowledge of themselves—the whole range of Christ's earthly and heavenly life, from his first advent to his second coming, is thus food for meditative thought.[84] To be sure, Jesus' life from annunciation to apocalypse presents a vast array of topics. Aelred thinks this variety helpful, indeed necessary: "Truly, since in this sad life there is nothing stable, nothing lasting, and humans never stay in the same state, it is necessary, while we live, that our soul be fed with some variety."[85]

Aelred is sure that meditation on Christ is of inestimable assistance in progress toward the perfection of happiness. The first step toward that happiness is the perfection of the intellect in knowledge, a knowledge made accessible through consideration of the humanity and human activity of the Son.[86] And meditation on Christ's humanity will lead the patient human to a much higher mode of consideration:

Surely, brothers, it is a great good and a great joy to know our Lord Jesus Christ in his humanity, to love him in his humanity, to view, as if looking into our heart, his birth, his suffering, his wounds, his death, and his resurrection. But a much greater joy will they have who can say with the apostle: "And if we have known Christ in the flesh, now we know him so no longer [2 Cor 5:16]." It is a great joy to see how our Lord was laid in a manger, but it is a far greater joy to see how the Lord reigns in heaven. It is a great joy to see him nursing at the breast, but it is a much greater joy to witness him feeding all. It is great joy to see him embraced by a little girl, but it is a far greater joy to see how he holds together the heavens and the earth.[87]

Meditation on this world, and on Jesus present in this world, will lead to a contemplation of him in the next that will, in part, fulfill the need and desire for happiness of which all humans are—or should be—aware. In that world, "like eagles soaring on their wings through the highest heavens, they are lifted high in contemplation to gaze on the near splendors of that sun seen by their unblinking eyes."[88]

V

Love: The Perfection of the Will

As essential as the perfection of the intellect is for Aelred, that perfection in humility is only a first step in the journey of a people pursuing happiness. Aelred writes, in a sermon on the Assumption: "...If some folk seem to be humble—in their dress, their food, and their attitudes—yet within are bitter toward their superiors and their peers,...humility cannot defend them from their enemies."[1] What is true of humility is true of all virtues and good deeds: they are efficacious in the pursuit of happiness only to the extent that they are informed by love. Better said, no human power is virtuous without love, no human deed is good unless done out of love. Aelred says it best: "...In it [love] is the perfection of all virtues. ...Nothing should be called virtue which this root has not brought forth; no work which has not ended in love should be thought perfect. In love are expressed both the fulfillment of the law and evangelical perfection...."[2]

Aelred is sure that the pilgrim folk seeking their homeland of happiness will find it by following the path of love, "in which consists the perfection of [one's whole] way of life...."[3] Love is a process, the goal of which is nothing short of perfection: "...I shall seek you, O Lord, seek you by loving you. Whoever makes progress in loving you, Lord, surely seeks you; whoever loves you perfectly, Lord, is one who has already found you."[4]

Loving is so central to Aelred's search because his universe is informed by God's love: "This love sustains and contains all creatures, leaving nothing in disarray, nothing in disorder, nothing without some appropriate plan and peace. Love is the heat of fire, the cold of

57

water, the clarity of air, the opaqueness of earth. Love binds and joins
all these quite opposing elements in all corporeal creatures...."[5]
Since the existence and order of all creatures are informed by God's
love, Aelred can see love in all of them:

> I see...in all creatures, even those irrational or insensate,
> some trace of love, by the fact that they are compounded of,
> and united from, diverse parts and opposing and inimical ele-
> ments. If love's likeness appears in other creatures too, surely
> its truth operates in the minds of the rational. So love is
> common to God, angels, and humans. So love, extending
> out to whatever is outside [one's own] nature, binds nature
> to nature, so that they may be of one heart and soul [see Ac
> 4:32], of one faith, one hope, one love.[6]

The law of nature is thus the law of love, and Aelred sees all nature
immersed in a sea of love.[7] He sees himself—and all other human
beings—capable of, and engaged in, a truly divine activity: love.

A. TRUE AND FALSE LOVE

What is this love of which Aelred speaks? He answers that to love is
to choose or to will.[8] Aelred describes the act of loving or choosing
in two ways: as true love *(caritas)* or as false or self-centered love
(cupiditas).[9] Aelred writes, in the *Mirror of Love:* "Truly, since that
power of our soul, commonly called love, is capable both of true love
and self-centered love, this love is obviously divided, as if by opposing appetites caused by new infusions of true love and the remnants
of its old self-centeredness."[10] True love is the key to happiness,
Aelred asserts, and false love dooms one to misery. He puts this suc-
cinctly in one pregnant sentence: "True love raises up the soul to
that for which it was made, but self-centered love degrades it to what
it was sinking of its own accord."[11]

The events or circumstances of human life are not the sources of
happiness or unhappiness. It is one's reactions to those events or cir-

cumstances that determine one's bliss or misery—reactions that Aelred describes as true or false loves. He offers several concrete examples: "Why is it that, when two people are sitting at the same table and have the same food set before them, one rejoices and the other grumbles? Why is it that, when two suffer the same injuries, one is cast down into self-pitying inertia while the other is filled with wondrous delight? When two are simultaneously stricken with the misfortune of bereavement or poverty, why is it that one blasphemes and the other gives thanks?"[12] For Aelred it is abundantly clear from observation of human reactions that external events and situations are not the source of one's true condition. It is rather one's internal disposition, one's true or false choice, that affects one for good or ill.[13] Clearly, for Aelred, true love is the key to happiness; false love dooms one to unhappiness.

But what is true love? What is false or self-centered love? Aelred explains in a sermon for All Saints day: "Self-centered love is present whenever you love anything other than God, and your neighbors because of God. We ought to love God because without him we cannot be happy, our neighbors because with them we can be happy. If we love anything else in this world, it is a matter of self-centered love, and this is like a sort of 'plank in the eye [Mt 7:3–4]' of the heart which impedes our vision of God."[14] To be true, love must be directed toward that which will bring one happiness. False love is a self-defeating love in which one chooses what will bring only unrest and despair. Aelred knows that the quest for true love, the rejection of self-centeredness, is a life-long struggle.[15] Yet struggle one must, for the will that wants its own way, and chooses to love self-centeredly, blocks the way to the true happiness that it seeks.[16]

For those who seek the path to perfection, the first step in their search must be the rejection of false love, for this "worldly love brings forth pride, seduces the senses with carnal delights, imposes the distress of anxiety for the body, shackles one with the burden of carnal habit and self-centeredness, and [thus] impedes the perfection of the divine commands."[17] True love, on the other hand, is the necessary prerequisite for happiness, as Aelred asserts in a sermon for the feast of the apostles Peter and Paul: "Where there is no inequity, no crookedness, no deformity or perversity, there is tranquility. This tranquility can exist only in true love . . . ."[18] In another sermon honoring those same saints, Aelred equates true love with the purity of heart that rejects the false love of worldliness.[19] Happiness is thus to be found only in the tranquility and purity that true love brings. In his *Mirror of Love,* Aelred contrasts this happy fruit of true love with the confusion and uneasy dissatisfaction resulting from misdirected love:

> What about you, my soul? Are you content going round and round in this perplexing circle? . . . What, I ask, is the gain of this labor? Anything other than the husks of swine [see Lk 15:16]? There is no satisfaction in this. If there is any satisfaction at all, then how much? How much more pleasant, more agreeable, more gratifying is the hunger of true love than the satisfaction of self-centered love! Surely, in terms of happiness there is no comparison. The more one is stuffed full with self-centeredness, the more empty one is of truth— and, hence, more miserable.[20]

True love perfects the choices of the will, and so the development of a rightly oriented will is crucial to happiness. But the growth of the will in true love also involves the participation of the intellect.

Love, whether true or false, is a choice made by the will. But the humans who employ their wills in choosing must have some notion of what they are choosing. Thus the intellect's knowledge is necessary to the choices humans make, to the sort of love they choose, and to the freedom with which they make their choices.[21] The intellect must also inform humans of the means they must embrace to accomplish what they choose.[22] Therefore, for Aelred, the intellect is clearly a necessary partner of the will in the love that will perfect the human being. Although the attachment of the *affectus* may be present in true love, it is not a necessary component of that love. The delight sometimes felt in true love is not essential; love is not an emotion but a choice.[23]

B. The Body's Role in Love: Good Deeds

True love requires the activity of the whole person, and this means that the body must contribute its share to the whole. That contribution is in the body's activity, the accomplishment of good deeds. True love is, and must be, expressed through good deeds. In a sermon on the blessed Virgin, Aelred makes true love golden clothing for both soul and body:

> Would that our soul might be clothed with gold of the deepest yellow, so that true love might "cover a multitude of sins [1 Pt 4:8]," for, as gold surpasses all other metals, so true love surpasses all other virtues. This gold is [also] applied to all our [bodily] parts: to the hand, that it might be open in giving freely but closed in receiving; to the eye, that, seeing its sister or brother in need, tears might flow and remorse might be aroused; to the tongue, that the ignorant might be instructed, the sad might be comforted, and the desperate might be cheered; to the foot too, that it might run to the aid of the falling brother or sister and stand by him or her when he or she is being ridiculed. The ear too is decorated [with gold], that it might hear the cry of the poor and their requests might not be scorned. The interior organs are not slighted; rather, the heart is so filled with true love that it has compassion [for others] and overlooks [their faults] out of loving-kindness.[24]

The body thus becomes the will's agent in translating its love into action.[25] Indeed, Aelred thinks, good deeds are a valid test of whether the will's love is true or false.[26]

The good deeds that express true love are legion, thinks Aelred, and they are of two sorts. The first is obvious: ministering to the needs of another. Aelred presents a heroic example in the person of Queen Mathilda of England, offered from a story related to him by King David of Scotland:

> "When I was a lad, serving in the [English] royal court," he said, "I was in my room with my friends one night, doing I

know not what, when I was called by the queen to her chamber. When I got there, I found the place filled with lepers, and the queen standing in their midst. When she had taken off her cloak and had furnished herself with a linen towel, she poured water into a basin and began to wash the lepers' feet and wipe them dry. When the feet were dry, she took them in both her hands and kissed them with devotion."

Astonished at the queen's behavior, David asked her:

"'What are you doing, my Lady? Surely if the king knew of this he would never consent to kiss your mouth, now polluted with the disease of these leprous feet.' Smiling, she answered: 'Who does not know that the feet of the eternal King should be preferred to a mortal king's lips? Indeed, I called you here, my dear brother, so that you might learn from my example to do the same....'"[27]

Not all are called to such heroism, Aelred knows, nor do many have the opportunity. Good deeds can be done, however, even for those whom one cannot meet—or, perhaps, even know—through prayer, which Aelred holds to be an efficacious way of expressing love. He asks a recluse: "What service can you give to your neighbor?" Aelred answers for her:

Nothing is more precious than a good will, says a certain holy man [Gregory the Great]. Let this be your offering. What is more useful than prayer? Let this be your abundant gift.... Look, then, on the afflicted and oppressed and have compassion for them. Call to mind the wretchedness of the poor, the sighs of orphans, the desolation of widows, the sadness of the suffering, the needs of strangers, the perils of sailors, the longings of virgins, the temptations of monks, the anxious care of prelates, the labors of those serving as soldiers. Open the heart of your love to all; offer your tears for them; pour out your prayers for them.[28]

Everyone has an opportunity to express love through good deeds, though the means may vary widely. Thus, "those who do nothing are like the bad, lazy servant who, having accepted [his lord's] money, buries it in the ground [see Mt 25:18]—practicing no fraud in accepting it but also gaining no accumulated profit."[29]

C. LOVE FOR ONESELF AND FOR OTHERS

"Truly," Aelred says, "if we examine the matter [of love] carefully, we find that humans must love these three: themselves, their neighbors, and God."[30] The first of these, love of self, receives relatively little attention from Aelred, for he sees it as self-evident. "...From the very nature of things," he writes, "all persons are dear to themselves."[31] Indeed, he says, "people ought to love themselves, as this is necessary...."[32]

Love of neighbor receives much fuller treatment. Aelred acknowledges that "we use the word neighbor in many ways: neighbor in location, in time, by nature, by blood, in likeness, in love, in mercy." He adds: "By nature,...all human beings are neighbors to all other human beings. It is in this sense that it is said: 'You shall love your neighbor as yourself [Mt 22:39].' That this is said of all humans, no Christian soul should doubt."[33] Aelred believes that love for others is also a matter of justice, but the ways he would express that just love show a warmth and sensitivity not usually associated with the word justice:

Justice grants each person his or her due....This, I would say, is an incentive to love of sister or brother, which begins by harming no one and grows by showing oneself without complaint against anyone. Through the charm of kindness, we win over many to ourselves. By our peaceful way of life we shall offend no one: we should be submissive to our elders, conciliating with our peers, and considerate of our juniors. To the first we should show respect and reverence, to the second honor and graciousness, to the third humble compassion.[34]

Compassionate love should extend even to the wicked, as did David's for Absolom. "It was good [of David]," says Aelred, "to wish to die in the place of the wicked [Absolom; see 2 Sm 18:33], so that he might live to repent, live to weep, live to receive God's mercy, lest he perish forever [see Jb 4:20]."[35] Aelred makes no distinctions based on worthiness; he teaches that all people should be loved and cared for, even to the point of one's being willing to lay down one's life for them.

Love for others need not take such an extreme form, and most often does not. And Aelred deals with a much more common response to one's neighbors, the anger which they arouse. Love takes a different form in this case, the form of restraint: "When anger arises, I advise that we not say more than is necessary. . . . By silence anger is crucified. How? Take up the keys of God's precepts. . . . Who is there who cannot crucify his or her tongue with these keys so that it cannot move?"[36] It is out of such small acts of kindness that Aelred sees constructed a perfection of self in love for others:

If . . . we direct ourselves to the haven of our heart, where we are wont to "rejoice with those who rejoice, to weep with those who weep [Rom 12:15]," to be weak with those who are weak, to burn with those who are scandalized [see 2 Cor 11:29], and we sense there our soul united in the bond of true love with the souls of all our sisters and brothers— there troubled by no prick of envy, inflamed by no heat of indignation, not wounded by darts of suspicion, not consumed by the voracious gnawing of melancholy—then we can clasp all our neighbors to the bosom of our utterly tranquil mind. There we can embrace and caress all with tender affection and make them of one heart and one soul [see Ac 4:32] with ourselves. Then, at this most delightful taste of sweetness, the tumult of all self-centered desires is quieted, and the clamor of vices is calmed. Within, there is an absolute freedom from all that is harmful, and, in the delights of love for our human siblings, there comes an agreeable, a joyful rest.[37]

Aelred is convinced that love for others is the way to one's own happiness. But, Aelred teaches, love will not be complete, happiness will not be obtained, if one ignores love for God.

D. LOVE FOR GOD

Love for God is the proper human response to the love that God has showered on all creation: "...[God] did not create anything to meet his own needs, but so that he might satisfy his overflowing love."[38] God's love is shown not only in creation but also in showering on humans the good things of that creation. In thanksgiving Aelred prays: "'You cover the heights of heaven with waters [Ps 103:3]' from which, by hidden waterfalls, you send down rain on the soil of our hearts, so that they may produce plentiful harvests of grain and wine and oil [see Ps 4:8], that we might not seek our bread in futile toil, but seeking might find [see Mt 7:7], and finding might eat and taste how delightful you are, O Lord [see Ps 33:9]."[39] God's goodness is the expression of his love; indeed, Aelred says to God: "...You yourself are love *[amor]*; you are true love *[caritas]*."[40]

In giving humans his love, especially in the gift of himself in the Son, God initiates a loving relationship of the greatest intimacy. "So," says Aelred, "we ought to love him in such a way that, when we see Christ coming from heaven 'with his angels [Mt 16:27],' we may not fear his coming, but instantly run with great longing to him, as to a most intimate friend."[41] God should be loved, Aelred thinks, in Christ's humanity as well as his divinity—with the ardor that Peter and Paul showed in their love:

> In the love with which Peter loved the Lord we are shown what delightful attachment we ought to have to the humanity of Christ. What fervor and love...Peter had for Christ's humanity we can demonstrate from the gospel....When the Lord spoke with his disciples about his passion and told them that he must be handed over and put to death, Peter loved him so tenderly and felt his bodily presence so delightful that

he said: "It would be better for you, Lord, not to allow this [see Mt 16:22]." ... But in Paul we are shown that love which we ought to have for Christ's divinity. He himself says: "If we have known Christ according to the flesh, now we know him so no longer [2 Cor 5:16]."[42]

Peter and Paul show Aelred the intensity of the love for God that humans can and should have. This love, Aelred thinks, is the highest virtue and encompasses all others. The commandment to love, Aelred is certain, "is broad, for it fulfills in itself all the other precepts.... As Scripture says: 'You shall love the Lord your God with your whole heart, your whole soul, with all your strength [Dt 6:5; Mk 12:30].'"[43] But if loving God requires one's whole attention, and all one's powers, how can one also have the intention, time, and energy to love oneself and one's neighbor?

E. THE RELATIONSHIP BETWEEN THE LOVES

There is no doubt that sometimes Aelred sounds as if love for God were so important as to limit severely, though never exclude, one's love for self or neighbor. For example, in his *Mirror of Love*, Aelred says of Jesus that "he alone among all, he alone above all, both captures our attachment and impels our love. He claims for himself a seat in the abode of our heart, not only the best seat but the highest, not only the highest but the innermost."[44] If "he alone ... impels our love" were to be taken literally, it is difficult to see how Aelred could allow a place in the human heart for love of self or others. But, of course, Aelred would not have us read him so narrowly.

Quite the contrary, while insisting that love for God is essential to human happiness, Aelred makes love for neighbor an essential expression of love for God: "Those who would love God will love also their sisters and brothers [see 1 Jn 4:21].... Jesus admonishes: 'This is my commandment, that you love one another as I have loved you [Jn 15:12].'"[45] Loving one's neighbor is thus one way to love God. So too is love for oneself.

In the third book of Aelred's *Mirror of Love,* he summarizes his teaching on the relationship of the three mandated loves in three densely constructed sections. In the first, he affirms the necessity for all three forms of love.[46] From this Aelred goes on to explicate the precedence he assigns to each of the three loves:

> So, in a way, love of neighbor precedes love of God. It pre-cedes it, I say, in order, not in excellence. It precedes that perfect love of which is said: "You shall love the Lord your God with your whole heart, and with your whole soul, and with your whole mind [Mt 22:37]." To be sure, some part, though not the fullness, of this perfect love [of God] neces-sarily precedes love of self and of neighbor, for without it both these loves are dead and therefore non-existent.[47]

Aelred then builds on the image of lifeless loves by seeing the love of God as their life-giving principle:

> It seems to me that love of God is a sort of soul to the other loves. It lives in itself most completely. Its presence communi-cates to the others their vital being; its absence brings their death. So that we might love ourselves, the love of God is formed in us; so that we might love our neighbor, our heart is, in a way, enlarged. Then, as this divine fire grows gradually warmer, it wondrously absorbs the other loves, which are rather like sparks, into its fullness. Love for God leads all our loves to that sublime and ineffable good where neither self nor neighbor are loved for their own sake—save that both are set free from themselves and completely carried off into God.[48]

Finally, Aelred descends from this ecstatic height to return to the mutually enriching relationship between the loves:

> Meanwhile, these three loves are engendered by one another, nourished by one another, inflamed by one another. Then they are all brought to perfection together. However, it

[sometimes] happens—in a wondrous and ineffable way—
that, though these loves are possessed together—for it could
not be otherwise—they are still not always sensed equally. At
one moment rest and joy are sensed in the purity of one's
own conscience. At another, they are derived from one's
delight in loving sisters and brothers. At still another, they
are more fully attained in contemplation of God.[49]

In the end, therefore, there is no tension for Aelred in urging aban-
donment to love for self, neighbor, and God. One can cheerfully love
one's neighbor as oneself, for "above all, God, who provides the
grace for a life of good deeds, is himself a neighbor."[50]

F. THE FRUITS OF LOVE

Loving God and one's neighbor leads humans along the path to happiness. Love, Aelred is sure, overcomes all one's failings: "It extinguishes inordinate desires; it abolishes anger; it drives out pride and
expels all vice. It darkens the eyes, so that they will not be curious; it
extinguishes all carnal sensation, so that we can say with Paul: 'I live,
but now not I, for Christ truly lives in me [Gal 2:20].'"[51] The will is
thus purified of vice: its choices are correct, and it directs the body in
the right use of its powers.

But the will is not the only faculty perfected by love: "If the soul
would only robe herself completely with true love, that love would
surely re-form the other two [faculties], memory and intellect, which
we have said were equally deformed [by the Fall]."[52] And Aelred
does not forget the effect of true love on the *affectus,* which in love
is filled with delight and joy.[53] Loving God also brings peace and the
rest Aelred describes as a sabbath: "Those who love you, [God,] rest
in you. Here is true rest, here true tranquility, here true peace, here a
true sabbath for the soul."[54] However, the peace that love brings as
refreshment to the journeying pilgrim on the path to happiness is but
a preparation for its fulfillment at the end of the journey: "This is
peace, which is a kind of foretaste which will feed you on the way,
and fill you completely in your homeland."[55]

Aelred is a teacher of love. He is also a great lover, who believes a life of love is a happy life. As he says in his treatise *On Spiritual Friendship,* "...You will not deny that he or she is most happy who rests in the inmost hearts of those among whom he or she lives, loving all and being loved by all, whom neither distrust divides nor fear casts out from this most serene tranquility."[56] Aelred counts himself among those thus happy. He recounts his experience in his monastery at Rievaulx:

> The day before yesterday, as I was walking around the monastery's cloister, the brothers were sitting around it, forming a circle of the greatest love. I marveled, as if in the midst of the delights of paradise, with the foliage, flowers, and fruits of each single tree around me. In that multitude I found no one whom I did not love and who, I felt sure, did not love me. I was filled with such joy that it surpassed all the delights of this world. Indeed, I felt my spirit poured out into all, so that I could say with the prophet: "Behold how good and how delightful it is for brothers to dwell together in unity [Ps 132:1]."[57]

VI

Friendship and the Perfection of Attachment

Although Aelred is sure that true love brings delight and joy, peace and serenity, to the affective powers of humans,[1] he also sees the *affectus*—and thus the whole human—fulfilled in friendship. Friendship requires love but is not the same thing as love—not even true love. Aelred does make an attempt to relate friendship and love by etymological derivation: "'Friend' *[amicus]* comes from 'love' *[amore]*, the nourishment of which is wisdom, and wisdom, as it 'reaches powerfully from one end to another' by its strength, so, by true love, 'disposes all things delightfully [Ws 8:1].'"[2] But, though they are related linguistically—and in the order of reality—Aelred is convinced that love and friendship are distinct.

In Aelred's treatise *On Spiritual Friendship,* he has Ivo, one of the participants in the dialogue, ask: "Are we to believe that there is no difference between true love and friendship?"[3] Aelred answers:

By no means! Not at all! Divine authority ordains that many more must be received into the bosom of true love than into the embrace of friendship. For we are compelled by true love's law to receive into the embrace of love not only our friends but also our enemies [see Mt 5:44; Lk 6:27–35]. But we call friends only those to whom we do not fear to entrust our heart and whatever is in it, to those who, in turn, are bound to us by the same law of faith and freedom from fear.[4]

Though quite different in the extent of their embrace, friendship necessarily proceeds from love: "The fountain and source of friendship is love. Though there can be love without friendship, friendship without love is impossible."[5] But all whom one loves are not friends, not even all those to whom reason and attachment direct one: "We embrace many with great attachment, but we still do not admit all of them to the intimacy of friendship, which consists above all in the revelation of our inmost thoughts and plans."[6]

The core of Aelred's complex, and sometimes confusing, concept of friendship is intimacy, itself a notion perhaps more easily described than defined. And Aelred does indeed describe its components:

> Four things seem especially to pertain to friendship: love and attachment, freedom from anxiety and delight. We see love in the benevolent giving of service, attachment in the delight which somehow springs forth from within, freedom in the revelation, without fear or suspicion, of all confidences and concerns, delight in the pleasant and amicable sharing of everything which happens, whether joyful or sad, the sharing of all thoughts, whether harmful or useful, the sharing of everything taught or learned.[7]

The attachment of the *affectus* is clearly a major component of the intimacy associated with friendship, but it is not the only element.

There are many sorts of attachment, Aelred says, some spiritual, some rational, some irrational, some dutiful, some natural, some physical.[8] Although attachments are in themselves good, each of them can have good or bad consequences. He writes:

> There is a [sort of] spiritual attachment which comes from the devil, a [kind of] irrational attachment which fosters vice, a [sort of] physical attachment which leads to vice. Not only should these [kinds of] attachment not be pursued, they must not be allowed. Still more, they must be uprooted from our hearts as much as possible. But the spiritual attachment which comes from God must not only be allowed but

stimulated and increased in every way. . . . Even our actions should surely be stimulated by this [sort of] attachment, but those actions ought not to be ordered according to this attachment.[9]

Attachments, then, need ordering, and the actions that spring from attachments need some moderating influence. This is because attachment "very often ignores moderation, does not properly gauge human strength, consumes physical passions, rushes blindly and impetuously toward the object of its desire, thinks only of that for which it longs and disdains everything else."[10] Because the *affectus* is the passionate, emotive faculty, "in undertaking some burdensome, arduous, and impossible task as if it were a slight and effortless work, it does not sense the troublesome afflictions to its outward person because of the delight of its interior attachment. . . . So that we might not overstep the bounds of physical capabilities, we must be restrained by the moderating influence of reason."[11] Thus, reason must regulate the *affectus* and allow the will to choose what is best for the whole human being. The intimacy of friendship can thus be ordered toward human happiness. "For that reason," Aelred writes, "the beginnings of spiritual friendship must have, first of all, purity of intention, the instruction of reason, and the restraint of moderation . . . ."[12]

A. Becoming a Friend

Because friendship and intimacy are such elusive constructs, listing their necessary components is not enough. Perhaps the best way to understand Aelred's teaching on friendship is to follow his description of the process by which one becomes a friend. In that process, the attachment of the *affectus* plays an initiatory role:

This inclination of the soul which we call attachment sometimes results from sight, sometimes from hearing, and sometimes from dutiful service. When we see persons with cheerful faces, a pleasant manner, delightful speech, we are immediately inclined toward them by an agreeable attachment. We sense in them some praiseworthy virtue and holiness. The same occurs in us when we anticipate some mutual service.[13]

The resultant inclination toward friendship, Aelred is sure, should not always be pursued: "Granted that attachment most often precedes friendship, still it ought not be followed unless reason leads it, integrity regulates it, and justice rules it."[14] In this triad Aelred finds the principles by which he and his hearers can select some for friendship from all those whom they must love, and from the smaller body of those whom attachment suggests:

> Not all whom we love should be received into friendship, for all are not found suitable for it. "Since your friend is the comrade of your soul, to whose spirit you unite, devote, and so share your spirit that you become one instead of two; and since you entrust yourself [to your friend]" as if "he or she were another you," from whom you keep nothing secret, "from whom you fear nothing," you should surely first consider whether he or she is suitable for all this . . . .[15]

Having found someone so suited to friendship, "then he or she must be tested and at last finally admitted."[16]

Aelred's testing process is rigorous and demanding—understandably so, given the degree of intimacy Aelred associates with friendship: ". . . The friend's loyalty, integrity, and patience must be tested. Little by little should occur the sharing of confidences, the serving of common concerns, and a certain conformity in outward expression."[17] Clearly, Aelred thinks that the conformity of friends' minds is suitably expressed in the external, physical likeness of both. It is equally clear that the unity he seeks is primarily spiritual. Thus "intention too must be tested. This is especially necessary since there are many who see nothing good in human affairs save that which eventually brings profit. These folk . . . lack genuine and spiritual friendship, which ought to be sought for its own and God's sake . . . ."[18]

B. How to Be a Friend

Given cautious choice and testing of a friend, one maintains the friendship, Aelred teaches, by a joyful though exacting service that is extraordinarily beneficial to both friends:

> How salutary is it then [for friends] to grieve for one another, to toil for one another, to bear one another's burdens [see Gal 6:2], while each considers it delightful to forget oneself for the sake of the other, to prefer the will of the other to one's own, to minister to the other's needs rather than one's own, to oppose or expose oneself to misfortunes. How delightful friends find it to converse with one another, to reveal their concerns to each other, to examine all things together and come to one decision on all of them.[19]

This self-revelation, which is such a major component of friendship, requires, Aelred is sure, a relationship based on equality.[20]

And, of course, the knowledge of another's inmost thoughts requires a friend to exhibit dedicated loyalty.[21] To loyalty, Aelred adds generosity—both material and spiritual.[22] Underlying Aelred's list is a concern for the friend's physical and spiritual well-being—and a great sensitivity for the feelings of the friend:

> You ought so to respect the eye of a friend that you do nothing shameful or undertake anything of which it is unbecoming to speak. When you fail yourself in any way, the failure so overflows to your friend that you alone do not blush and grieve interiorly, but your friend too, who sees or hears of the failure, reproaches herself or himself as if she or he had failed . . . .[23]

Respect, concern, and sensitivity can be expressed in many ways. And indeed, Aelred teaches that one must support one's friend in all possible ways:

> There are other benefits in spiritual love, through which friends can be present and of advantage to one another. The

first is to be solicitous for one another, then to pray for one another, to blush for one another, to rejoice for one another, to grieve for one another's faults as for one's own, to consider each other's progress as one's own. By whatever means in one's power, one ought to raise up the faint-hearted, support the feeble, console the sorrowful, restrain the wrathful.[24]

Although prayer for one's friends is passed over quickly in this statement, in another passage Aelred makes clear the importance of prayer for friendship. There he underscores the efficacy of prayer for both the person praying and the one for whom the prayers are offered:

Added to these [practices of friendship] there is prayer for one another, which, in remembering the friend, is more effi-cacious the more lovingly it is sent to God with flowing tears brought forth by fear or awakened by attachment or evoked by sorrow. Thus, one praying to Christ for her or his friend, and for the friend's sake hoping to be heard by Christ, directs her or his attentions earnestly and longingly to Christ. Then it sometimes happens that, speedily though impercepti-bly, the one attachment carries over into the other, and, as if coming into close contact with delight in Christ himself, one begins to taste how sweet and sense how pleasant he is [see Ps 33:9; Ps 99:5].[25]

The practice of friendship thus leads one from an exalted human relationship to intimacy with the divine Source of friendship.

" . . . Among the advantages [of friendship] are counsel in doubt, consolation in adversity, and other benefits of like nature . . . ."[26] But, Aelred adds: " . . . Let us also correct one another, knowing that 'wounds from a friend are better than an enemy's deceitful kisses [Prv 27:6].'"[27] Correction, however, must be done in the right spirit; "the desire to dominate" must never be the corrector's motivation.[28] It is so important to friendship that correction be given without overbearing domination that Aelred makes his guidelines explicit. He first details the approaches to be avoided: " . . . Beware of anger and bitterness of spirit in correction, so that you can be seen to desire the improvement of your friend rather than the satisfaction of your own irritation. I have seen some who, in correcting their friends, cloak their upswelling bitterness and boiling rage sometimes with the name of zeal, sometimes with the word candor. Following impulse not reason, they do no good by such correction, but rather cause great harm. Among friends there is no excuse for this vice."[29] Rather, Aelred admonishes,

> a friend ought to have compassion for the friend, ought to reach out to the friend, ought to think of the friend's fault as his or her own, ought to correct the friend humbly and compassionately. Let a somewhat troubled countenance or saddened word make the reproof. Let tears take the place of words, so that the friend may not only see but also feel that the reproof comes from love rather than rancor. If the friend should reject your first correction, surely you must correct him or her a second time.[30]

The friend who corrects must also possess a sensitive insight into the personality and character of her or his friend, for there are some friends "who benefit from blandishment and quite readily and favorably respond to it. There are others who cannot be so guided and are more easily corrected by verbal chastisement. So conform and adapt yourself to your friend that you may respond appropriately to your friend's state of mind."[31] Finally, because correction must serve the truth, the corrector must not deceive his or her friend in the mistaken belief that this might serve their friendship: "A friend owes truth to her or his friend, without which the name of friendship can have no value."[32]

This is indeed a demanding program, though Aelred insists it is far more rewarding than burdensome. But the heavy demands that friendship imposes surely bring with them the possibility of failure, and Aelred recognizes this. When one has wronged a friend, Aelred's remedy is humble effort at reconciliation: "If it should happen that we neglect the law of friendship in some way, let us shun pride and seek to win back our friend's favor by some humble service."[33] If one has been wronged, Aelred urges the same sort of response: "...A friendship is proven more excellent and virtuous in which the one who has been hurt does not cease to be what he or she would be, loving the other by whom he or she is no longer loved, honoring the other by whom he or she is rejected, blessing the other who has spoken badly of him or her, and doing good to the other who has contrived evil against him or her."[34]

Intimacy is at once the way in which friendship is best expressed and the joyful fruit of friendship: "...Let those who are united to us by the delightful bond of spiritual friendship be happily hidden in the innermost and most secret recesses of our heart, be bound ever more tightly to us, and be more and more fondly cherished."[35] The delight, the joy, in this intimate relationship is, for Aelred, a means to the delight and joy experienced in an intimate relationship with God himself: "Surely our desire should be directed toward this: that in God we delight in one another, as is fitting, and that we delight in the God who is in both of us."[36]

C. The Foundation of Friendship

For Aelred, friendship is not merely a pleasant adjunct to human life; it is a reflection of a fundamental aspect of the ordering of the cosmos. Friendship is found among inanimate beings, among plants and animals, and among angels.[37] From the first moment of their existence on earth, human beings have been so constituted by God that they need the intimate companionship of one another to be truly human. For Aelred, the first models of friendship were Adam and Eve; in their natural, pristine state, humans exhibit the happy intimacy of husband and wife.[38] "As I see it," writes Aelred, "nature first impresses on the human mind the desire for friendship, then experience encourages it, and finally the authority of law regulates it."[39]

For Aelred, then, "it is evident that friendship is natural, as are virtue, wisdom, and the like—and it should be sought and preserved for its own sake as a natural good...."[40] Without the intimacy of friendship, happiness is impossible for humans. As Aelred puts it:

"Truly, even in those in whom wickedness has obliterated every sense of virtue, reason, which cannot be extinguished in them, has left a desire for friendship and fellowship, so that, without fellow human beings, riches can hold no charm for the avaricious, nor glory for the ambitious, nor pleasure for the licentious."[41] Aelred is sure that "without friends absolutely no life can be happy,"[42] and he offers the doubter this challenge:

> ... Let us suppose that the whole human race were removed from this world, leaving you as the sole survivor. Now behold before you all the delights and riches of the world: gold, silver, precious stones, walled cities, lofty castles, spacious buildings, sculptures and paintings. And now consider yourself re-formed into that ancient state in which all [creatures] are subject to you, "all sheep and cattle, all the beasts of the field as well, the birds of the air and fish of the sea which swim through the waters [Ps 8:8–9]." Tell me now, I ask you, whether without a companion you could be happy with all these?[43]

Even in this world—a world inhabited by great numbers of people— happiness is impossible unless one reaches out to some one of them in friendship: "If you were to see a person living among many others, suspecting all, fearing all as ambushers lying in wait to injure him or her, cherishing no one and thinking himself or herself cherished by none, would you not judge such a person wretched indeed?"[44]

This conclusion Aelred sees as so obvious, so grounded in nature and reason, that it is accessible to all who, through reason, recognize the natural order: "Even the philosophers of this world have ranked friendship not among matters casual or transitory but among those virtues which are eternal."[45] Perhaps the most forceful statement of Aelred's position is this:

> I should call them beasts, not humans, who say that one ought to live without being a source of consolation to anyone. Beasts even those who say that one ought not be a source of burden or grief to anyone. Beasts too those who

take no delight in the good fortune of another or bring
before no other their own bitterness at misfortune, caring to
cherish no one and be cherished by none.[46]

D. The Perfect Friendship of God

In Jesus of Nazareth, God shows himself as friend, and, in return,
Jesus must be loved as "a most intimate friend."[47] Aelred demonstrates his response to his own admonition in a sermon for Christmas: "At other times my office [as abbot] compels me to speak;
today attachment provides the necessity. But from where will the
words come to me? Surely, if my whole body were transformed into a
tongue, I could not satisfactorily express my attachment [for Christ].
No wonder! I have seen how great is he who comes for the salvation
of all people."[48]

Aelred teaches that friendship for Christ is possible only because
of Christ's friendship for his sisters and brothers. Indeed, their friendship with each other is informed by Christ's friendship and thus leads
to friendship with him:

> ... In friendship are joined honesty and delight, truth and
> enjoyment, charm and good-will, attachment and action. All
> these are begun by Christ, are advanced through Christ, are
> perfected in Christ. So the ascent does not seem too steep or
> unnatural, the ascent from Christ, who inspires the love by
> which we love our friend, to Christ, who offers himself to us
> as a friend to love—so that delight might follow on delight,
> enjoyment on enjoyment, attachment on attachment.[49]

Aelred offers a concrete and scriptural example of Christ's friendship
for human beings in the case of the family that lived at Bethany,

> where the most holy bond of friendship was consecrated by
> the authority of the Lord. For Jesus loved Martha and Mary
> and Lazarus [see Jn 11:5]. No one can doubt that this was
> because of the special privilege of friendship by which they

are said to have clung to him. Evidence for this is the kind tears that Jesus shed with those who were crying [over the death of Lazarus]—the tears that all the people interpreted as a sign of love: "See," they said, "how much he loved him [Jn 11:36]."[50]

For Aelred, then, "friendship is a step bordering on perfection, which consists in the love and knowledge of God, so that a human, from being a friend of a fellow human, becomes a friend of God, as the Savior says in the gospel: 'I shall now not call you servants but my friends [see Jn 15:15].'"[51] And thus Aelred can say that, long before that gospel passage was written, "Moses spoke with God as a friend with a friend...."[52]

Aelred thus affirms God's intimate relationship with humans, and the possibility of God's leading humans to friendship with him. And this leads Aelred to a statement that he acknowledges is daring. In the dialogue *On Spiritual Friendship,* Aelred has one the participants ask: "What is this? Should I say of friendship what John, the friend of Jesus, says of true love [see 1 Jn 4:16]: that God is friendship?"[53] Aelred answers: "That would be unusual and does not carry the authority of Scripture. Still, what is true of true love I do not really doubt can be said of friendship, since those who abide in friendship abide in God, and God in them [see 1 Jn 4:16]."[54]

Aelred clearly sees friendship as "a step toward the love and knowledge of God."[55] Friendship leads one to the contemplation of God in this world[56] and to union with him in the next.[57] And all these glorious fruits are, for Aelred, the product of God's initiative, often beginning in a conversation between potential friends. At the very beginning of Aelred's dialogue *On Spiritual Friendship,* he states simply: "See, here we are, you and I—and, I hope, a third, Christ, is in our midst."[58]

VII
The Path of Virtue

The perfection of the intellect in humility, of the will in love, of the *affectus* in friendship would seem to suffice for the happiness of human beings. But Aelred also offers advice on a parallel, complementary, and supportive path to human perfection in the practice of virtue. This path of virtue entails, of course, the uprooting of vice:

> Taking our start from Paul's words, we say that the root of all evils is self-centeredness [see 1 Tm 6:10], just as—to take the opposite tack—true love is the root of all virtue. So, as long as the poisonous root [of self-centeredness] remains in the depths of the soul, even though some of the small shoots [of vice] are cut back on the surface, others will inevitably sprout with renewed life—until this root, from which these ruinous shoots of vice spring up, is torn out completely and nothing more remains of it.[1]

Love is once more established as the foundation of progress—or the lack of it—in the pursuit of perfect happiness.

A. CONVERSION

The human mind, the human soul, indeed the whole human, must turn—or be turned—from the path of vice to that of virtue. The first step in this process is the mind's conversion from its mistaken view of what constitutes happiness: "The mind, immersed in the dung heap of fleshly pursuits and aspiring to nothing beyond the dregs of the senses, chooses as its firmly held goal either delusive riches or futile honors or bodily indulgences or worldly favors—any one of them or all of them together—in its mistaken beliefs which depict happiness as the attainment of such things."[2] But the conversion that follows is central to human progress, for it is the conversion of the will from self-centered love to true love. Aelred likens this conversion to circumcision: "There are two [sorts of] spiritual circumcision. The first, which took place at baptism, was doubtless a cleansing from all sin. The second, which took place in the truly perfect conversion of humans, was renouncement of all temporal things."[3] This circumcision, this conversion, is not only possible for people of all walks of life, it occurs daily in the life of the Church: "Do you not see every day the proud folk of this age turning toward the Lord in great confusion and with much anxiety? Do you not see them humble themselves and weep for their sins? Surely, brothers, this happens every day."[4]

To this point, Aelred's insistence on the necessity of conversion seems to imply that it is the human will and human endeavor that bring about conversion from vice to virtue. His words seem to indicate that, in conversion, humans turn themselves toward God. But that turning, Aelred insists, is ultimately a product of God's gift of himself in grace. Conversion, for Aelred, is not so much a matter of humans turning toward God as God placing himself forcefully in the path of human gaze in such a way that humans cannot ignore him, even if, in the end, they reject him. Aelred tells his monks this in a sermon for a feast of Saint Benedict: "You were held in bondage by your own self-centeredness; you were held captive by your evil way of life. Brothers, how could you be set free unless the Lord had struck him [your captor] down? How did he strike him down? Surely by the good will he gave you, by the good desires which he inspired in you, by the good thoughts which he sowed in your hearts."[5] Languishing in the darkness of self-destructive sin, the unhappy soul may call out for help, but her very cry for help is an echo of the cry for conversion with which God fills her ears and heart.[6] The voice that cries out in sinners is never still, Aelred is sure; so he urges them to listen, "so that they may never despair of his [Christ's] goodness, who so exercises judgment as not to forget mercy."[7] Sinners of all sorts are converted "by the gift of humility and penitence."[8] Of one of them, Saul of Tarsus, Aelred says: "Many sins were forgiven him [see Lk 7:47], not because he loved much but so that he might love much."[9]

God's unrelenting pursuit of humans, his unremitting efforts to win human conversion, are likened by Aelred to God's sexual conquest of a woman who has strayed: "When such a one is tormented and seduced by adultery, fornication, impurity, or other reprehensible vice, if our Lord should possess her and place in her his seed, she will then begin to fear on account of her sins, begin to ponder and resolve to set herself straight, so that she might seize on a better life. This soul is a woman whom the seed makes pregnant."[10] The pregnancy leads to a new life, in which the soul grows and matures in her conversion under the continued ministrations of the Spirit.[11]

Aelred is convinced that it is God who initiates the human journey on the road of virtue. Perhaps his best illustration of this conviction is his description of his own conversion. Aelred first describes his troubled pre-conversion state and the efforts God made to break through to him:

See, dear Lord, how I have wandered the world and [have seen] those things which are in the world. . . . In these I sought rest for my unhappy soul, but everywhere [I found] labor and lament, sorrow and affliction of spirit. You cried out, Lord; you cried out and called. You terrified me and shattered my deafness. You struck, you flogged, you conquered my hard-heartedness. You sweetened, you flavored, you banished my bitterness. I heard you calling, but, alas, how late . . . .[12]

But this was, for Aelred, only the beginning of his conversion. Though he was still strapped to his sinful state, God's call led him to a consideration of his condition:

I lay rotting and covered over, bound and captive, entangled in the bowels of stubborn sin, crushed by the burden of long-established habit. So I directed my attention to myself:

who I might be, where I might be, what sort of person I might be. I shuddered profoundly, Lord, and was sorely afraid of my own effigy. I was terrified before the horrid image of my unhappy soul.... Had you not quickly extended your hand, I, who could no longer tolerate myself, might perhaps have been brought to the worst remedy: despair.[13]

Thus brought by grace-filled self-reflection to the brink of despair, Aelred began to recognize and to turn toward the Source of true happiness. He tells us: "I began, little by little, to savor you with taste-buds still not quite healed. And I said: 'Oh, if only they might become still healthier!'"[14]

But the struggle was not yet over. Aelred's mind may have been turned toward God, but the force of his passions held him back—until he was overcome by God's grace:

I was seized up to you, but I fell back into myself again. Those things which I sensed with delight through the flesh held me, as if shackled, by the force of habit.... Whatever I looked at became worthless to me, but habitual carnal pleasure held me fast. But you who "hear the groans of those in shackles," you who "release the children of the slain [Ps 101:21]," broke open my chains. You, who offer your paradise to harlots and tax-collectors, converted me, the worst of all [sinners], to yourself. See how I breathe [easily] under your yoke, how I rest [easily] under your burden, for your yoke is pleasant and your burden light [see Mt 11:30].[15]

Aelred sees himself converted by God to God, the action of God requiring only a will that, under the inspiration of God's grace, does not reject that conversion.

B. RESTORATION

Conversion places the pilgrim on the road to virtue, and thus to happiness. The first restorative steps on that road, Aelred affirms, are contrition—which he also calls repentance or penitence or compunction—confession, and purgation—also called penance or satisfaction. The words are different and the order often varies, but the basic pattern remains consistent. Pilgrims must unburden themselves of the weight of the past so they can proceed with greater freedom. And this, Aelred knows, requires humility: "The proud do not repent, do not lament, do not make satisfaction. Descend, like Naaman, from the chariot of your pride [see 2 K 5:14]. Cleanse yourself through confession; wash yourself through compunction; heal yourself through satisfaction. So descend to inner contrition, to wash yourself seven times [see 2 K 5:14], to come forth to confession, to works of satisfaction."[16]

1. Contrition

Contrition requires a humility in which fallen humans see themselves as they truly are and mourn over what they see: "... They mourn so that they may merit the remission of sins which follows. Then they mourn so that they may be consoled by hope for the divine promises. ... O delightful and desirable mourning, through which the dead are raised, the sick healed, the blind enlightened, the doors of heaven opened."[17] For Aelred, this mourning is salutary indeed: "The food for the soul's health is compunction; as the prophet said: 'You will give us food in the bread of tears [Ps 79:6].'"[18]

Compunction is also a means by which the soul is purged through remorse "from the memory of its wantonness, as if from a filthy morass of dung."[19] This filth is swept clean by the "sweeping broom" of contrition.[20]

2. Confession

Confession also plays a crucial part in the pursuit of perfect happiness:

> The first hour is considered, fittingly indeed, the one of our conversion, in which we "cast off the works of darkness and put on the armor of light [Rom 13:12]." The confession of sins we say is the third hour, for confession ought to be of

three sorts of sin: of thought, of speech, and of deeds. Or it
could be considered the third hour because confession will
suffice if the heart is contrite, the mouth confesses, the body
is reduced to [its proper] value.[21]

Aelred sometimes indicates that the "confession which cures"[22]
should be sacramental. In a story about a sinful and despairing nun to
whom a holy prelate appeared in a vision, Aelred relates that the
bishop said: "You are responsible for this [suffering], for you have not
yet acknowledged your sin to your spiritual father as you should. See
to it that you confess as quickly as you can, and take this from me as a
command, that you chant psalms to Christ each day."[23] But most
often Aelred's confession is extra-sacramental, an acknowledgment
before God of one's self-destructive behavior. For example, in a sermon for Advent, he writes: "True love 'will cover a multitude of sins
[Jas 5:20]';... when our daily confession [of them] and continual satisfaction [for them] are made apparent in the sight of God, those sins
are hidden from the eyes of his majesty."[24] Whether sacramental or
not, Aelred sees confession as most efficacious, sometimes expressing
his confidence in rather earthy language: "The door of penitence is
like a dung-gate, through which the filth of sin is expelled by the
sword of confession."[25] But the most important component in
Aelred's confidence is his trust in the loving response of God to confession: "Crimes are voluntary and must not only be brought to a
reckoning but also punished. But both are remitted by God's loving-
kindness if a complete confession and a worthy satisfaction follow."[26]
Reliance on God's love infuses even this rather legalistic formulation.

3. Purgation

Still, for Aelred, "satisfaction" is not so much the paying of a legal
penalty as it is a means of purging oneself of past sin and thus progressing in the spiritual life:

Those who have openly committed shameful acts are in need
of [equally open] lamentation, so that, as the magnitude of
their sins has not been hidden, their true conversion might

not [also] be hidden. For those who, puffed up with pride, trumpet forth their sins like Sodom [see Gn 18:20], it is necessary that they descend to weeping, so that, just as in sinning they ascended the mountain of passion, they might descend in humility to the valley of lamentation.[27]

Purgation also has a didactic purpose; it aids in the development of that humility, which, in turn, leads to still greater virtue: "... Those who are in any way wise, who are converted to the Lord, 'will make their way from virtue to virtue [Ps 83:8],' from self-knowledge to penitence, from penitence to humility, from humility to purity."[28] Those thus converted and sent forth on the path to virtue are Christ's crowning glory.[29]

But the crown of conversion is won only at a price—not only the price of Christ's passion but also the price paid by the one converted. Conversion—and the contrition, confession, and purgation necessary to it—involves a painful struggle, a process Aelred likens to a difficult birth: "There is a spiritual birth when the sterile and unfruitful soul conceives by fear of the Lord. By conversion to the Lord, good works begin to be born. What pain is there in this birth when the flesh, by the will's habit, resists the spirit, when the mind wants this passage yet fears it, is driven through this passage by delight in the good yet is held back by the desire for evil." Still, Aelred assures us, the emergence of the child called conversion brings a joy that erases from the memory the pains of birth.[30] Aelred employs a complementary image, growth from childhood to adolescence, to illustrate the process of conversion. Aelred first describes the behavior of sinners whom he compares to wicked children: "Whenever humans are so stupid that they give themselves over to vice and sin, they neither care nor think about God or about anything which might call them back from their wicked ways, but they freely do what they like without any quarrel heard from their heart or conscience. They are children with no [sense of] discretion."[31] "But," adds Aelred, "whenever such folk begin to ponder their condition and consider their wickedness and sin, their own conscience begins to speak against them and to restrain them. Then they begin to think about this life's end, to mull over what awaits them if they should perhaps die—and thus they begin to be afraid. When this fear takes hold of their heart, they begin to withdraw themselves from their wickedness and to live under the yoke of fear."[32] "This," Aelred concludes, "begins their adolescence, in which they begin to resist vice and sin and be steadfast in facing the devil and his suggestions. In this state, under this yoke, there is labor and tribulation, and humans begin to sense what the Lord said in the gospel: 'How narrow is the way which leads to life [Mt 7:14].'"[33] This is but a beginning; a sincere conversion, although attained through God's grace and by intense effort, is but a stage in the development of a mature and happy human.

C. THE FOUR PRINCIPAL VIRTUES

Scattered throughout Aelred's many lists of virtues are repeated references to a quartet of virtues that he sees as fundamental to the attainment of spiritual maturity. He insists that "through temperance we are pure; through prudence we choose the good and reject evil; through justice we love God and neighbor; through fortitude we persevere in all these goods."[34] "These," Aelred says, "are in fact the four virtues which are necessary for all . . . ."[35]

These four virtues are not only necessary for all people, they also support other virtuous activities, such as friendship, which "prudence directs, justice rules, fortitude guards, and temperance moderates."[36] Thus, Aelred asserts, these "are the four virtues which are the food for all the other virtues, and their starting places . . . ."[37]

Prudence is a virtue of the intellect: "The head of our soul is our mind, which is the seat of reason and the adornment of which is surely prudence. Folly disfigures the mind so adorned . . . ."[38] Prudence is the virtue that recognizes the good and directs one in the proper pursuit of it.[39] Prudence can also distinguish between the good and the better, between the bad and the worse.[40] One who recognizes and distinguishes these Aelred calls wise.[41]

Although prudence is a virtue of the intellect, it also has a powerful impact on the will. Prudence points out the way that the will must follow: "With prudence one knows what to love and what not."[42] Prudence also directs the *affectus,* so that one is not led astray

by one's attachment—even though that attachment may be legitimate and understandable. Aelred offers the example of

> ... "Rachel, weeping for her children, [who] refused to be
> consoled [Jer 31:15; Mt 2:18]." Why did she weep? Attach-
> ment. Rachel's attachment would be consoled if her son were
> recalled from death, if the mother were to delight once more
> in the sight of him. But Rachel did not want this. Why?
> Because if he were recalled from death, he would be cast down
> from bliss into misery. She did not want her son recalled but
> rather that she be taken up into rest with him. Attachment
> sought her children, but reason withstood attachment. Divine
> providence delayed the mother's assumption, and so "Rachel,
> weeping for her children, refused to be consoled."[43]

Prudence is important for the body as well. The body's virtuous
activities must be governed by discretion; humans must be "discerning, so that they may not overstep moderation in their actions...."[44]
Without the moderating force of prudence, humans suffer from an
ignorance "that does not observe the proper measure in their good
and laudable activities. This ignorance knows that abstinence is a
great good, but ignores any moderation in this good.... Discretion... enlightens the eyes of the heart in all matters. As the Lord
says in the gospel: 'If your eye is darkened, your whole body will be
darkened [Mt 6:23].'"[45] Prudence thus moderates the virtuous
actions of the body, and so the entire human being benefits from the
virtue of prudence. As a consequence Aelred counsels: "... Learn the
virtue of discretion and pursue [good] counsel, thus gathering much
for your well-being, for your progress in many ways...."[46] Aelred
can thus happily claim for the discretion of prudence that it is "the
mother and nurse of all the virtues."[47]

The virtue of temperance is closely related to that of prudence,
and it seems to involve the ability to apply prudence to the concrete
realities of daily living. "... Temperance moderates,"[48] says Aelred,
and insists that "some moderation must be observed sensibly by all,
and must not be exceeded by any one in any way."[49] Aelred explains
what this moderation of temperance means: "The apostle seems to

have suggested in a few words the right attitude toward the life of
perfection when he said: 'Let us live soberly and justly and uprightly
in this world [Ti 2:12].' Sobriety is a sort of moderation in human
life; it is the temperance which prudently avoids excess and leads us
on our course along the royal road [of virtue], wavering neither to the
left or to the right."[50] Temperance thus cools the ardor of "those
who, . . . unreasonably following all the violent impulses of their
attachments, become feebler rather than holier."[51] It also moderates
and directs their desires for material or physical satisfaction. The needs
of the body and of physical existence are, for Aelred, clearly legitimate
and must be honored.[52] And the passions are to be regulated, not
suppressed: "Happy the soul . . . in which the bridle of moderation
regulates these [passions] . . . ."[53] Through temperance "we maintain
in ourselves some measure and moderation, so that we are not devas-
tated by having less than what is necessary, so that we are not brought
by a pernicious presumption to possess more than we should."[54] It is
in this sense that Aelred can urge his readers to "pay attention, not to
what the flesh suggests, but to what reason dictates . . . ."[55]

Those virtuous activities that regulate the passions must themselves be regulated by temperance: ". . . The outward practice of
virtue—about which it is said: 'Do not be overly righteous [Qo 7:17]'—
must be tempered by the moderation of reason."[56] With temperance, as with all else in the life of virtue, the object is true love.
Temperance, Aelred believes, must "restrain and dull the enticing
impulses of body and spirit, lest the soul, so seduced, prefer the
delights of culpable pleasure to the pleasure of loving one's sisters and
brothers . . . ."[57]

Although Aelred's notion of justice includes the proper ordering
of one's own faculties,[58] his emphasis is clearly on the justice due to
others—to God and neighbor.[59] As temperance serves one's own
needs, "so justice serves our neighbors. . . . Among our neighbors
there are those who are above us [in authority], those who are our
equals, and those who are below us. So if we wish to live justly, we
must accord our superiors our humble submission and obedience,
our equals honest love and reciprocating respect, our inferiors kind
compassion and caring thought."[60] Justice thus requires discernment
of the needs of others and a loving response to the needs discerned.[61]

As "true love gives birth to justice,"[62] so "through justice we love God and neighbor...."[63] The apparent paradox is resolved for Aelred when he reflects on the nature of both love and justice:

> If you contemplate quite deeply the rules of justice, no one does more to give each its due than the one who loves what he must love as much as it ought to be loved. That is, God above oneself, one's neighbor as oneself—God for himself only, oneself and one's neighbor only for God. You see, if I am not mistaken, that the perfection of justice depends on the perfection of true love, so that justice seems to be nothing other than well-ordered love....[64]

Aelred knows that the virtues of prudence, temperance, and justice are not easily attained or maintained, but he is confident that "through fortitude we persevere in all these goods."[65] Fortitude makes one "strong, lest some temptation divert one from one's purpose...."[66] Fortitude gives one the "constancy of heart and tranquility of mind" that enable one to "guard oneself courageously against all vices which arise."[67] All the hardships that the pilgrim encounters on the path to happiness are to be met with fortitude.[68] Thus, Aelred says: "...Fortitude supports one in adversity,...the fortitude which, I think, can be not incongruously compared to a sword belt with which a very powerful man habitually girds himself when launching an attack."[69] The life of virtue is a struggle; for Aelred the battle is won only by those who employ the weapon of fortitude.

Fortitude requires will-power, or, to put it another way, fortitude is a virtue of the will. But to be strong, the will requires the cooperation of the intellect: "...Fortitude without wisdom is foolhardiness, and wisdom without fortitude is weakness."[70] Indeed, to make human choices and actions completely effective, the *affectus* must also contribute to the cooperative effort of the will and the intellect:

> Wisdom without fortitude is weak; fortitude without wisdom is blind. This is because we are able to know from wisdom what should be done, but without fortitude we are not able to do what should be done. Again, through fortitude we are

able to do what should be done, but without wisdom we are not able to know in what way it should be done. Still more, wisdom without delight is cleverness, and delight without wisdom is stupidity. Similarly, fortitude without delight is foolhardiness, and delight without fortitude is negligence. Through the pairing of wisdom and fortitude, we work effectively, but, if we work without delight, we shall surely be miserable in this work.[71]

Fortitude may be a difficult virtue, requiring burdensome effort,[72] but that effort should not be sad.

Aelred offers the promise that the life of virtue will bring perfection to the humans who live it. He believes that the happiness thus promised is well worth the effort expended in following with fortitude the path of perfection: "If we wish to possess this [perfect] peace at the Lord's second coming, we must acknowledge his first coming 'with faith and love [1 Tm 1:14].' We must persevere in the works which he displayed and taught, thus nourishing us with his love and true desire. With these may we run to meet him 'as perfect humans [Eph 4:13]' when he comes to judge the world. . . ."[73]

D. The Practice of Virtue

Those whose conversion is being accomplished are ready, Aelred thinks, to set out on the path of virtue. Their restoration has begun through contrition, confession, and purgation. Their lives have been oriented correctly through the four principal virtues of prudence, temperance, justice, and fortitude. But they must have places on the path to set their feet; they must have a way to walk. So Aelred offers a host of virtuous practices that will help pilgrims find their way on the path, help them journey toward the happiness they seek.

1. Silence and Solitude

Curiously enough, one of Aelred's admonitions to pilgrims pursuing their goal is leisure in that pursuit.[74] Aelred's leisure is not, however, the leisure of idleness but the leisure of freedom from distraction, a tranquility experienced in silence and solitude.[75] Aelred acknowledges that, when he wishes "to meditate quite clearly and penetratingly, all the bodily senses are great hindrances to me, so much so that the quiet silence of the night appeals to me. I often close my eyes [when meditating], lest other [sensations distract] me."[76] Thus, concludes Aelred, "the first need for one longing for spiritual meditation is quiet...."[77]

Aelred offers two more reasons for the virtue of silence. The first stems from his knowledge of the tongue's power for evil:

> There are many who have honey in their mouths but not a dripping honeycomb [see Sg 4:11]. They possess many sweet words, but these do not come from an abundance of sweetness. In some ways they are like bees, which possess sweetness and also a sting. On one hand, they possess honey because they speak sweetly, flatter everyone, attend to the desires of all. But this is all outward show. Privately, or perhaps in their hearts, they sting, secretly, with detractions and judgments, those whom they have besmeared outwardly with honey.[78]

Silence, Aelred is confident, is capable of curbing the untamed tongue.[79]

Aelred also knows from experience the power of silence to speak to Christ. In admonishing a recluse he says she is to

> sit alone and keep her mouth still, so that her spirit might speak. And she must believe herself never alone when she is solitary. For then she is with Christ, the Christ who would think it unseemly to be with her in a crowd. She must, therefore, sit alone and keep silent, listening to Christ and speaking with him. She must curb her tongue, first being intent on speaking rarely, then being intent on what she speaks, and, finally, taking care with whom and how she speaks.[80]

Lest one think Aelred's prescription for silence is intended only for solitaries whose calling demands silence, Aelred adds: "If this [counsel] is applicable to any respectable person, how much more does it pertain to a recluse."[81]

Aelred knows that silence is a difficult virtue, even for those who have chosen to walk the path of virtue within the cloister. In one of his sermons, *On the Burdens of Isaiah,* Aelred includes this ironic and instructive passage:

> You know, brothers, that silence burdens and is a heavy load for many.... Their head aches, their stomach rumbles, their eyes water, and their kidneys almost let loose. All these [symptoms] disappear, however, through noise and talk, and all is [once more] pleasant, sorrows are forgotten, all the body's parts return to their [normal] function. How great is the power of the tongue, which can [thus] clear the eyes, alleviate headaches, control the kidneys, strengthen weak knees![82]

Aelred believes that silence truly brings many solid benefits to those who curb their tongues: "... The Lord says through the prophet: 'On whom shall my Spirit rest if not on the one who is humble and peaceful' and who 'trembles at my words [Is 66:2]?' This is a most holy state of mind, but foolish talk, even too much talk [see Prv 10:19], destroys it, so that you see there is nothing you should pursue more than silence."[83]

Perhaps the best model of the sort of silence that Aelred counsels is himself. Gilbert of Hoyland, a fellow Cistercian, would write of Aelred after his death: "He was lucid in interpretation, not hasty in speech. He questioned modestly, replied more modestly, tolerating the troublesome, himself troublesome to no one. Acutely intelligent, deliberate in statement, he bore annoyance with equanimity."[84] Gilbert also offers a concrete example of Aelred's silence in speech: "I remember how often, when someone in his audience rudely interrupted the course of his teaching, he stopped speaking until the other had fully exhausted his breath. When the gushing torrent of untimely speech had abated, he would resume his interrupted discourse with the same serenity with which he had waited, for he both spoke and kept silent as the occasion demanded."[85]

If silence can be found in speaking, for Aelred it is also true that solitude can be enjoyed in the company of others. Aelred writes: "There are . . . [solitary folk] who live physically among [other] people but inwardly possess great tranquility and great peace; they are devoted to purity of heart and the contemplation of God. They are solitaries in spirit."[86] Interior solitude need not mean living apart, as the scene in the garden of Gethsemane shows Aelred: "He [Christ] withdrew to a place more hidden, although taking with him Peter and the two sons of Zebedee [see Mt 26:37] . . . ."[87] But Aelred also acknowledges that all people can profit from seeking tranquility in some physical isolation, in which they can search for ". . . Him whom we now find in the forest's meadows [see Ps 131:6]."[88] In at least occasional physical withdrawal from the hurly-burly of everyday life, "the soul flies up . . . from solitude to knowledge, through knowledge to wisdom."[89] Still, the true meaning of solitude for Aelred is not physical separation but a spiritual detachment from one's physical surroundings: ". . . What does it mean to have entered 'into solitude [see Ex 8:27]'? It means to hold this whole world as a desert, to long for the homeland, to possess only as much of the world as what suffices for this progress on the path, not as much as the flesh desires."[90] Solitude thus becomes simplicity.

2. Simplicity

Simplicity is shown in those who cut off all distractions from their goal of true happiness: "Just as the hairs of the body are more than abundant, so they are bald who renounce superfluity, content with those things which are necessary."[91] Aelred does not counsel rejection of all things of this world; but he does insist that the virtues of prudence and temperance should inform one's choices of material things. ". . . In the use of legitimate things," Aelred counsels, "some moderation should be observed. In eating or drinking one should restrain oneself from overeating and intoxication. In [possessing] riches one should do away with anxious preoccupation [with them]. In conjugal acts one should avoid shameful passions. In choosing clothing one should seek utility, not expense."[92] In seeking to be simple, one should consider not only one's own needs but those of others, especially "those cast down into need."[93] Thus, in the practice of simplicity, the intellect must employ its power of discretion, and the will must respond to the demands of true love. Simplicity also requires an honesty in assessing the body's needs—an honesty difficult to obtain and maintain, but apparently within reach of the soul that heeds the virtuous intellect and will.

Aelred's simplicity also demands a realization of the distinction between one's physical condition and one's spiritual state: "There is a poverty of the flesh, and there is a poverty of the spirit. Poverty of the flesh is the possession of insufficient means. Poverty of the spirit is the voluntary humbling of mind and body for God.... 'Blessed,' then, 'are the poor in spirit [Mt 5:3]' whom the Lord fills with the spirit of awe [see Is 11:3] and, through that awe, nourishes love."[94] From this it is clear that Aelred distinguishes between poverty and simplicity—though he sometimes uses the word "poverty" for "simplicity." When poverty is the "possession of insufficient means," it is clearly an evil, not a virtue; thus Aelred can ask: "Who is there who does not see that poverty, grief, hunger, and thirst are no small part of [human] misery?"[95] Yet the poverty of spirit that is simplicity is indeed a virtue:

> "And the first-born of the poor shall be fed, and the poor shall rest with confidence [Is 14:30]." These are the poor of whom the Lord says: "Blessed are the poor in spirit, for theirs is the kingdom of heaven [Mt 5:3]." This poverty is determined by attachment, not by external appearances. Thus [David], one abounding in riches and with the highest royal authority, says: "Truly needy and poor am I [Ps 69:6]."[96]

Spiritual poverty, or simplicity, is thus not the lack of physical possessions but the possession of the right attitude toward them.

Aelred does not condemn wealth, but he is convinced that those who possess it have an obligation to use it for the well-being of others.[97] Thus "alms-giving fosters loving-kindness, so that one can keep oneself from cruelty...."[98] But, Aelred warns, the wealth of the world is dangerous: "As long as one heeds and holds the riches and honors of the world, one can perhaps be humble, but one's humility is not [very] apparent."[99] Nevertheless, the proper use of wealth can promote the true love that leads to happiness.

3. Obedience

Like nestlings watched over by their father and nourished by their mother, all humans must heed the admonitions of those who care for them. In this they but follow the example of the young Jesus in response to his caring—and sometimes grieving—parents.[100] The sensible response to this sort of care, Aelred is sure, is to heed those wiser in the ways of the spirit, those who have traveled the path of virtue.[101] For Aelred, obedience is a rational response to the love and care with which others offer their help and direction in the pursuit of perfect happiness.

Obedience is also a reflection of the need of any society to order itself in the pursuit of the common weal:

> ...The greatest care must be given not to exceed the pre-scribed way of life in any [social] arrangement whatever. It is evident that some folk must be in charge, some must be sub-ject [to the authority of others], some must be equals [in authority]. Thus, whenever any one of these folk oversteps the proper bounds, one who is subject [to his or her author-ity] ought to mention this to [his or her] superior, one peer should correct another, and a superior should even, if neces-sary, rebuke a subject. Surely the suggestion or correction or constraint must be adapted to the nature of each individual, so that submission may be experienced in the suggestion, love in the correction, compassion in the constraint.[102]

Obedience is thus a means of ordering all societies; it is also a reflec-tion of the spirit of justice that must inform all spiritual striving.[103] But Aelred's notion of justice is always closely tied to his compas-sionate concern for others.

So Aelred's obedience is not an unthinking acquiescence to the will of another; it is the rational response of those seeking perfection to the counsel of those who have traveled far along the path that all should seek to follow. Aelred returns once more to the example of the youthful Jesus: "... He comes into the temple as a boy, learning, not teaching, listening and asking questions—and in all this not withdrawing himself from the oversight of his parents. Thus, Lord, thus do you lead the way for the unfortunate, thus do you heal the sick. This is the way you point out to the wandering, this the ladder for the climbing, this the return route of exiles."[104]

4. Chastity

Exiled pilgrims, returning to their homeland, must tread their path in chastity. Aelred is convinced that "it is necessary that they consecrate themselves to God through the virtue of chastity."[105]

For Aelred, chastity is a virtue that encompasses much more than restraining the body's sexual urges: "Chastity of the flesh is present when one distances oneself voluntarily from illicit kisses, from defiling embraces. There is chastity of the senses when all the bodily [sense] organs restrain themselves from all illicit pleasures. Spiritual chastity is present when one expels all unclean attachments and drives all impure thoughts from the eye of one's heart . . . ."[106]

The intellect, will, and *affectus* are all active in the virtue of chastity, and the purity of heart that results leads to bodily purity, a transformation into a condition that anticipates that which the body will assume in the life to come.[107] Again, it is not the passions of the body that are the obstacle to virtue; it is rather the self-defeating choices of the will that cause the body to produce evil.[108] Jesus is Aelred's exemplar in purity of heart, and he is likewise the goal of that purity: "Above all, it is necessary that one imitate the nakedness of Christ through the renunciation of worldliness, and so, through chastity, prepare the soul and body that they might be worthy to be the dwelling-place of Christ."[109] Chastity, purity of heart and body, is thus incumbent on all who would seek and find the happiness of perfection.

But Aelred also recognizes that some are called to a chastity entailing more than that of those "who do not exceed the limits of marriage...."[110] There are some "who, declining to propagate [offspring] by the free [exercise of] the flesh, castrate themselves for the kingdom of heaven [see Mt 19:12]...."[111] This metaphorical castration consists in their voluntary renunciation of the pleasures of sex and family life in order to concentrate their efforts on the inner life of virtue.[112] But, Aelred insists, this form of chastity is not required of all:

> This is a voluntary sacrifice, a spontaneous offering, to which no law impels one. No necessity compels one; no commandment impels it. This the Lord says in the gospel: "The person who can take hold of it, let that one take hold of it [Mt 19:12]." Who can do this? Surely the one in whom the Lord would inspire it, the one to whom he grants the power. First of all then, O virgin, you must commend your good resolution, with the greatest devotion of your heart, to him who inspired it, entreating him with most earnest prayer that what is impossible to you by nature you might observe easily through grace.[113]

All who pursue the virtue of chastity are imitators of Christ, but those who choose to renounce marriage follow him in the special form of chastity that he himself adopted.[114]

Aelred appreciates the anxiety of those who find chastity difficult, those who are tempted and fear their own fall. But he is cautious about the remedies that some administer to themselves. By way of instruction, Aelred tells the story of a monk who "feared his chastity was imperiled by the impulses of nature.... So he aroused himself against himself and, conceiving a most monstrous hatred for his flesh, sought nothing more than that which would afflict it." Afflict it he did, emaciating "his body through fasting, ... plunging himself frequently into frigid waters, ... [and rubbing] his body with nettles." Aelred reports that "all this was insufficient, and the spirit of fornication harassed him no less...."[115] Punishment of the body is not Aelred's answer to the assaults of unchastity, whether real or created by an overly sensitive and scrupulous conscience. Aelred relates that the monk, realizing the inadequacy of his own efforts, turned to Christ for assistance: "...He prayed, wept, sighed, pleaded, and begged, prostrate before the feet of Jesus, imploring him either to kill him or to heal him. [Finally]...he was so completely filled with the delight of chastity that he conquered all the pleasures of the flesh which can be felt or imagined."[116]

Aelred knows that chastity is a virtue necessary to progress on the path to perfection. But, he affirms, "proud chastity is no virtue, because pride, which is in itself a vice, makes everything thought to be a virtue conform to itself [in vice]...."[117]

5. Prayer

Pilgrims on the path to perfection find support for their journey in prayer. Aelred sees prayer as a many-faceted activity. For him as a monk, and for many others, one of the most important means of prayer is the formal liturgical prayer that centers on the psalms. Although liturgical prayer is formal and structured, it is to be prayed with an ardor stemming from deep attachment and burning love.[118]

But this love and attachment Aelred would have his hearers express through other prayerful activities as well, through reading, private prayer, and meditation.[119] Aelred urges a balanced life of prayer, employing common-sense alternations. He urges a recluse:

> Impose on yourself no fixed rule for the number of psalms [you recite], but, as often as the psalms please you, use them. If they begin to be a burden, change over to meditative reading. When meditative reading engenders distaste in you, rouse yourself to prayer. When wearied of all these, take up manual labor. By this healthy alternation you will refresh your spirit and banish spiritual weariness.[120]

Aelred shows his common sense too when speaking of the recluse and the length of time she should spend in prayer, saying that "she ought to prolong or shorten [her private prayer] as the Holy Spirit guides her. She should take care, however, that more extended prayer does not engender a distaste for prayer. It is more profitable to pray more often and more briefly than once for a too prolonged time— unless, of course, it be prolonged, without one's recognizing it, by the inspiration of devotion."[121]

Prayer is not easy, Aelred knows, and those who pray also know how hard it is to pray with devotion:

> In whom, I ask, is there the power to pray as she or he wishes? Do we not suffer from the same inadequacy whether we wish to be dissolved in tears or boil up with devotion, have our confidence bolstered, be enkindled with the flame of love, or be lifted up in contemplation? You should know from experience that none of these lies within your power. But God sends the Spirit of his Son into your heart. . . . It is he, present in the hearts of the praying, who pours forth healing lamentations, so that even to the lamenting it can be said without error that he speaks for us.[122]

In prayer Aelred thus sees himself not so much as one who speaks to God as one in whom God speaks to God. This sort of speaking has important consequences: "Prayer even increases good works; devotion is enhanced [by it] and love aroused."[123] And, during the penitential season of Lent, he counsels the good soul to "devote herself more frequently to prayer, prostrate herself more often at Jesus' feet, and by the frequent repetition of his most delightful name, arouse compunction, call forth tears, and curb her heart from all distraction."[124] Prayer is indeed, for Aelred, a strong staff that gives support to those on the journey to virtue.

VIII
The Happiness of Perfection

The path that spiritual pilgrims follow culminates in the happiness of perfection, the goal that has motivated them to begin and pursue their arduous travels: "...What is more fitting for a rational creature, if just, than happiness...?"[1] Aelred is confident that those who follow the path he describes will wend their way out of the land of unlikeness and be re-formed in the likeness of God: "Virtue...and its reward, happiness, constitute the land of likeness, vice and wretchedness the land of unlikeness.... The more one is filled with vice, the less like God one is, and, consequently, the farther one is from God. But the greater one's virtue, surely the greater one's likeness to God and the nearer one is to him."[2] So close is the perfected soul to God that Aelred can speak of the relationship as the highest form of marriage.[3]

This union is, for Aelred, the result of God's loving initiative.[4] Of course, the happiness of a virtuous life requires a response from the folk who seek it. But that response need only be a reliance on the loving-kindness of him who leads them to that happiness—a reliance that will lead them to "repose in the delight of virtue."[5]

A. THE PROCESS OF PERFECTION

For Aelred, perfection is a process, a journey that is accomplished in the happiness of love and that aims at the state of happy rest. Aelred writes: "We must not forget that, in the formation and re-formation of our nature, true love is reckoned to be, so to speak, in motion....

When the creature is perfected by the contemplation and love of God, it is said, without doubt, to stand immovable."[6] This journey involves leaving the land of unlikeness to travel toward the happy "mountains of virtue."[7] Aelred offers a brief itinerary for the three-stage trip:

> .... Let us, who have begun to turn to God, bring that conversion to its perfection. Let us start out from Joseph, where our growth begins. Let us progress and ascend until we pass through "the deportation to Babylon [Mt 1:17]," so that we—who, because of our vices and sins, have been prisoners under the power of Nebuchadnezzar in Babylon [see 2 K 24:14], in confusion, that is—may be set free through the grace of Christ, to whom we have turned.[8]

The second stage Aelred describes in terms of ascent to God:

> And so, when we have returned from Babylon [see Ezr 2:1] by our complete conversion to God, we may come quickly to the second stage. Beginning there to cleanse ourselves, let us ascend step by step until we come to Solomon, the peacemaker, so that, cleansed of evil passions, we may possess some peace and tranquility. And thus we enter the third stage with David the "desirable," so that, we too may long and burn to see the desirable face of our Creator. In this our longing we have come to Abraham, to the Father on high, that we may see "the God of gods in Sion [Ps 83:8].'"[9]

The paradox of perfection, its simultaneous search and attainment, its beginners who are at the same time perfected, is well expressed in one of Aelred's sermons on the Epiphany: "Happy the soul which so loves, is so afire, that she searches everywhere for God and repeats what has been written: 'In all I have sought rest [Si 24:11].'"[10] The contrast between the state of happiness and the process of search is clear. But, I think, this contrast serves not merely rhetorical purposes; it is a reflection of what is for Aelred a profound reality: the "state" of perfection is, in this life, the "process" of seeking perfection.

This is because, for Aelred, the "perfection" attained in this life always contains at least some small "admixture of imperfection—whether of pride, of vanity, of a taste for human praise, or indeed, through the stealing into our conversation of something less than discreet."[11] It would seem that Aelred thinks the most perfected human still has some faults. Though humans can receive and achieve, even in this life, a likeness to God, there always remain in them some distracting traits: "... She [the soul] possesses a certain blackness [see Sg 1:4] in her own tent on account of the temptations which she suffers and because of the ill-regulated desires of the flesh not yet perfectly subdued. But still she is 'beautiful like the tents of Solomon [Sg 1:4].'"[12] Relying on this beauty, Aelred urges his audience to act in as perfect a way as possible—in striving for peace, for example:

> Although we cannot perfect this peace in this life, still we ought to act in this life as if we were peacemakers, making peace between ourselves and our neighbor, between our body and our soul, between ourselves and God. For "blessed are the peacemakers, for they will be called the children of God [Mt 5:9]." Those who strive to create this peace in themselves, who strive to win the war against vice and the temptations of enemies, receive now some likeness to the Son of God, who is the true peacemaker, who has destroyed the devil and reconciled human nature to God. But we cannot create this peace or win the battle against vice and the temptations of enemies unless the Lawgiver gives his blessing [see Ps 83:8], unless he who teaches us what we ought to do gives us the strength to do what we wish.[13]

Perfection thus remains a process, but a process blessed by God's grace.

So Aelred encourages the "perfect" to continue to respond to God's perfecting action in them: "The apostle seems to have suggested in a few words the right attitude toward the life of perfection when he said: 'Let us live soberly and justly and uprightly in this world [Ti 2:12].'"[14] This requires a continuing effort to be prudent:

"The Lord says in the gospel: 'Who, wishing to build a tower, would not first sit down to ponder whether he or she could afford to finish it [Lk 14:28]?' This tower is the perfection to which we ought to ascend."[15] Perfection, then, is a condition of continuing conversion in this life.[16]

B. The Perfection of Body and Soul

The happiness of perfection can be received and achieved, Aelred says, in all the faculties of the soul—in the intellect, will, memory, and *affectus:*

> What could be more delightful, what could be more glorious, than, through disdain for worldliness, to perceive oneself raised high above it and, by standing on the summit of a good conscience, to have the whole world at one's feet! To see nothing for which one longs, no one whom one fears, no one whom one envies, nothing of one's own which could be taken away by another, no evil which could be inflicted by another on oneself![17]

This freedom combines detachment from the world and attachment to God.[18] And the glorious freedom that Aelred sees in perfection overcomes the evil to which both body and soul are subject:

> What, I ask, is more delightful and what more tranquil than not to be tempted by the turbulent impulses of the flesh, not to be set on fire by the flames of carnal incitement, not to be stirred by any seductive sight? What is more delightful than to possess a body cooled by the dew of modesty and subject to the spirit, a body no longer seducing one with the enticement to carnal pleasures but most obedient to spiritual practices? Finally, what is so near to divine tranquility than not to be moved to inflicting abuse, not to be frightened by any torment or persecution, to possess the same constancy of mind in prosperity and adversity, to view with the same eye

both foe and friend, to conform oneself to the likeness of him "who causes his sun to rise on the good and the bad and his rain to fall on the just and the unjust [Mt 5:45]"? All these exist together in true love, and all exist together only in true love . . . .[19]

Clearly the will and its correct choices in love are central to Aelred's concept of perfection.

That love must not be lukewarm. Its perfection in ardor is the soul's first task, and so, "if one is wicked and cold, one should conceive [a sense of] awe, and through awe ascend from the coldness of iniquity to the heat of true love."[20] This process of purification will lead to an essential love, the love of self: ". . . First we sweat profusely at good deeds, and then at last we can pause in tranquility of conscience. From good deeds is born purity of conscience, by which standard love of self is judged. For just as those who do or love iniquity do not love but hate their own souls, so clearly those who love and work for justice do not hate but love their own souls."[21] And love of self will lead by the difficult path of virtue to love of others: "So all must purify themselves, allowing nothing within themselves which is unbecoming and withdrawing themselves from nothing useful. Loving themselves thus truly, they should follow the same rule in loving their neighbor."[22] This arduous journey will culminate in the love that reflects one's growing likeness to God, for "a certain likeness to God shines forth in the virtues."[23] The ardent love thus received and obtained leads, Aelred is sure, to the soul's "foretaste of that for which she has longed, of that to which she has aspired, of that for which she has sighed in this her pilgrimage."[24]

Perfection in love requires perfection of the intellect, for the intellect must discern the good that the will can then love.[25] The process of perfecting the intellect also requires arduous effort,[26] for it requires that the mind be "meek that she may learn humbly, meek that she might not unreasonably resist [instruction]."[27] Those who are meek in mind and humble of heart become the friends of Christ and gain from that association knowledge denied to others.[28] The joy experienced in the knowledge granted to friends of God finds Aelred standing in wonder and awe:

But who is that soul which can say: "I shall hear what the Lord speaks in me [Ps 84:9]"? "In me," the soul says. There "stands the friend of the bridegroom"; there the soul "hears him" and "rejoices with joy at the bridegroom's voice [Jn 3:29]." O how deeply interior is this joy! All her glory is from within [see Ps 44:14]. There, within, there she rejoices at the Bridegroom's voice. Brothers, as you have heard that you are sharers in that rough life which John [the Baptizer] endured [see Mt 3:4; Mk 1:6], so [now] see yourselves sharers in that joy which is within, not outside. There, within, you should take care to hear the voice of the Bridegroom [speaking] to you, and rejoice at his voice.[29]

Perfection is possible in the *affectus* as well: "When someone acts not only out of [volitional and intellectual] agreement but with a certain attachment of love and delight of mind, then she or he lies in the marriage bed, as if in some interior embrace, . . . and there receives our Lord, Jesus Christ . . . ."[30] The joy experienced in the *affectus* responds to the whole process of perfection:

We are sentenced to a deplorable slavery [to sin] until, ourselves loving and forgiving, we are forgiven and loved—and not merely set free but made friends. Truly this is a time of peace, a time of quiet, a time of tranquility, a time of glory and exultation. For what troubles, what disturbances, what grief, what anxiety could tarnish the joy of those who . . . progress by a fuller grace to this state of divine likeness . . . ?[31]

The perfection of the *affectus* lies in both peace and joy[32]—and in the perfection of the friendship that adds so much to that peace and joy. For friendship "can . . . be perfect between the perfected."[33]

Aelred does not neglect the body's perfection. Through proper direction of its natural impulses, the body receives "a kind of incorruptibility [see 1 Cor 15:53], . . . a foretaste of some of the delight of the coming resurrection . . . ."[34] There is a kind of perfection for both body and soul, Aelred says, in simply bearing the everyday burdens of human life.[35] Aelred sees all these burdens gradually crushed and destroyed in the person being perfected.[36] Then, Aelred assures us, by fasting from vice and embracing good deeds, humans are perfected: "They pass over to the place of the wonderful tabernacle, up to the house of God, [singing] with the voice of exultation and praise, with the sound of solemn celebration [see Ps 41:5]."[37]

C. The Wondrous Harmony of Perfection

The perfected folk who sing with this voice "the sound of solemn celebration" will resound like a harmonious harp, whose "spiritual strings [are] stretched between two pieces of wood, an upper and a lower, prefiguring the mystery of the cross." On this harp Aelred hears the strings of the four fundamental virtues playing in harmony: "The first of these strings is temperance, through which one mortifying one's [physical] parts 'on the earth [Gn 1:11]' joins all to Christ. This string is fixed to the base of the cross, so that, founded in fear, it may emit the deep sound of confession and compunction." Aelred then turns his ear to "the second string, justice, [which] is attached to a higher part of the cross. In giving to each what is its due, it bursts forth with the brightest voice of true love. And the string of prudence, placed between the other two on the traverse wood of the cross, tempers the second string's keenness and the other's depth with the sweet sound of discretion." Aelred also hears a "fourth string, which is called fortitude [and] embraces the length of the cross, outstripping the others in the virtue of steadfastness and emitting the pleasant sound of patience. Truly, the strings of each of these virtues is joined side-by-side with the others, and these various sorts of several strings surely form, from numerical ratios, one spiritual harmony."[38] The harmony of virtuous perfection accords perfectly, in Aelred's mind, with the order of the universe and with the economy of salvation.

The perfection that results brings an unexpected harmony to the whole person:

Whoever you are, O soul, whom the compassion of God has freed from unhappiness, you have been given rest from your labors and troubles, and from the harsh slavery to which you have been until now subject. You are surely surprised at how very easy continence has become for you. You are astonished at having thrown off the yoke of ingrained habit—even to the point that your nascent desperation at the great effort needed to get rid of it has been removed. . . . Rejoice with trembling; cry out in astonishment: "How is it that the oppressor has ceased, that the tribute is spared [Is 14:4]?"[39]

Thus the harmony of the human with the divine,[40] and of each human with all others,[41] will sound forth in a music that is for Aelred the perfection of human life on earth: "If we persevere in this warfare and do not consent to vice, we shall have the kingdom of God within us in this life, that is, justice and peace and joy. Justice as a result of virtue, peace arising from the harmony of flesh and spirit—when they together agree on the good—joy from the testimony of a good conscience [see 2 Cor 1:12]."[42]

D. The Perfection of the Coming Life

The joy that perfected people experience in this world is as nothing when compared with the joys that they will experience in the next life. Speaking of the saints in heaven, Aelred says: "Now consider, brothers, if you can, how exalted are they in heaven who can be so exalted and honored on earth. Surely, brothers, if we could see, at one and the same time, all the glory of the world and all the praise of the world and all the joy of the world, in comparison with this joy of theirs it would seem nothing other than absolute misery."[43] Aelred is convinced that a place in this company of the saints awaits all who have traveled the hard road of virtue. Indeed, he often places such a reward before his audience in the hope of encouraging their efforts.[44]

Reward implies merit, and, since it is clear to Aelred that some folk are more meritorious than others, this brings up the question of whether the heavenly rewards are equal for all. One of the participants in Aelred's dialogue *On the Soul* puts the question this way: "Are there not some [blessed] souls more perfect than others, or are they all equal in perfection?"[45] Aelred answers:

... The Lord said: "In my Father's house there are many rooms [Jn 14:2]." He thus distinguished various degrees even among the perfect.... You know that, among the saints, there are distinctions of reward, just as of merit.... Each room [in the Father's house] has its own perfection. So each person is said to be perfect who, in differentiation from all others, is found ready for that room for which she or he has been destined.... So all will be equal in the same everlasting state, but different in the rooms [to which they are assigned]. So all will be equal in their happiness because, as one true love works its effect in them all, each will have what they all will have, and all will have what each one has.[46]

But these distinctions fade from Aelred's thought when he considers that all God's folk, in whatever way or to whatever extent, are perfect because they have been perfected by God's free gift of salvation; they are the people of Israel who are "the people belonging to God, clearly those who were predestined 'to life everlasting [Ac 13:48].'"[47] Thus, even those saints whose lives were characterized by exemplary spiritual and physical practices of virtue are, for Aelred, the recipients of celestial happiness, not the authors of it.[48] In his *Life of Saint Edward, King and Confessor,* Aelred states this position quite clearly by putting in the mouth of the dying saint these words: "...I go to the Father to receive the joys promised to the faithful. This is not for my merits but by the grace of the Lord our Savior, who has pity on whom he wills and shows mercy to whom he pleases...."[49] An appropriate, accepting response to God's loving-kindness allows the recipient a confident hope in everlasting happiness. Aelred prays: "May there be for us a spiritual resurrection when, progressing from fear to hope by a happy leap, and secure now in the remission of our sins, we sigh for that celestial good with a sort of mental rapture. Following our Lord, with our attachment and desire, in his ascension into heaven, let us now presume to sit with him in the heavens and reign with him."[50]

In heaven, Aelred is sure, the holy folk reign together with Christ—and with each other. He sees Saint Edward welcomed into the celestial realm by other saints, including Peter, John the Evangelist, and Mary, the mother of Jesus: "... The citizens of heaven came to meet him. The ethereal key-bearer unlocked heaven for him; the disciple whom Jesus loved ran to meet him. As a virgin, with that virgin he follows 'the Lamb wherever he goes [Rv 14:4].'"[51] Once welcomed, the new citizen joins the community of the saints in their common activities of praising God and caring for those left behind in the community of those still struggling to join them:

> Blessed Ninian, made perfect in life and mature in age, passed happily from the world and was borne to heaven, accompanied by angelic spirits, to receive an eternal reward. There, associated with the apostolic choir and added to the ranks of the martyrs, enlisted in the army of holy confessors and adorned with virginal flowers, he does not cease assisting those who hope in him, those who cry out to him, those who praise him.[52]

The prayer and care of the saints for those still striving on earth is, for Aelred, a reflection of the profoundly social nature of all humans, who, he thinks, cannot be happy save in association with others.[53] Thus, the saints in heaven "themselves care for our progress [in perfection], and they pray for us all the more devoutly as they know themselves incapable of perfection without us."[54]

Aelred's heaven is thus a community, a community that rejoices together and resembles nothing so much as a celestial banquet—prefigured, Aelred thinks, by Christ's eating and drinking with his friends and disciples on earth:

> ... After his resurrection our Lord wished to entrust great mysteries to us by means of certain physical signs. During those days he appeared to his disciples as they were fishing, and, at his bidding, they brought to shore "a net filled with large fish, one hundred and fifty-three [Jn 21:11]." This symbolizes those who, at the coming resurrection, will be presented to the Lord by the ministers of Christ. And that

meal which he wished to share with his disciples signifies that
banquet at which we shall, in his kingdom, eat and drink at
his table [see Lk 22:30].[55]

E. The Final Fulfillment

From that heavenly banquet nothing that fills and fulfills humans will
be missing. So splendid is the food of the heavenly banquet that it
transcends Aelred's intellectual powers and defies his imagination to
describe it: "What the nature of that kingdom [will be] is something
of which we cannot even think, much less tell or write. I do know
that nothing at all will be lacking that you might wish to have present, that nothing will be there that you might wish to be absent."[56]
Aelred seems to know much of what heaven is not, and, despite his
disclaimer, he knows much of what heaven is as well:

> So what are the goods there present? Where there is neither
> sorrow nor tears, what could there be but perfect joy? Where
> there is no tribulation or temptation, no variation in, or
> worsening of, weather, neither violent heat nor harsh winter,
> what could there be but the most moderate temperature
> and true and complete tranquility of mind and flesh? Where
> there is nothing for you to fear, what could there be but total
> security?[57]

Heaven is, above all, a state of immersion in the glories of true love,
for

> where there is no discord or envy or suspicion or any ambi-
> tion, neither adulation nor detraction, what could there be
> but supreme and true love? Where there is no poverty or any
> covetousness, what could there be but abundance of all good
> things? Where there is no deformity, what will there be but
> true beauty? Where there is no toil or weakness, what will
> there be but complete rest and vigor? Where there is no
> prospect of old age, no fear of disease, what could there be

but true health? Where there is neither night nor darkness, what will there be but perfect light? Where all death and mortality have been swallowed up [see 1 Cor 15:54], what could there be but everlasting life?[58]

That everlasting life and bliss are enjoyed by the whole human, both in body and in soul:

> ...[The body] will be full of the majesty of the Lord, who will give life to the dead, cleanse the impure, heal the infirm, glorify the ignoble, make the temporal perpetual. And, if this will be the coming happiness of the body, of what sort, I ask, will be the happiness of the soul? ...There will be occasion for our joy in the contemplation of the Creator in his creatures, of love for the Creator in himself, for the praise of the Creator in both.[59]

1. The Vision of Truth

"...In the Lord's land, ...no temptation will be able to gain access to the Lord's mountains, that is, to our spirits suspended in the excellent state of divine contemplation."[60] Those thus suspended "abide in the perfect vision of God."[61] They are like the virgin Mary, who "on the day [of her assumption] passed on from this world and ascended to the heavenly kingdom where she began to contemplate his [God's] glory, power, and divinity...."[62] They are like Mary too, who "see him 'face to face [Gn 32:30]' and dwell forever in the holy vision of him."[63] This, Aelred asserts, fulfills the gospel promise: "'Blessed are the clean of heart, for they shall see God [Mt 5:8].' That is, we shall see his divinity, that excellence and beauty, as the angels see it, for we shall be 'like the angels of God in heaven [Mt 22:30].'"[64]

Clearly this contemplation brings knowledge, and Aelred sees the intellect perfected in this vision: "There [in heaven] 'I shall know as I am known [1 Cor 13:12],' for there 'we shall see him [God] as he is [1 Jn 3:2].' 'Now we see in a glass but obscurely, but then face to face [1 Cor 13:12].'"[65] The vision of God, Aelred asserts, brings

great knowledge of him, for "he will be seen in himself, seen in all
his creatures, ruling over all without anxiety, sustaining all without
toil, sharing himself with and, in a way, dispersing himself to each
one according to his or her capacity—without diminution or division
of himself. That lovable and longed-for face, 'on which the angels
desire to gaze [1 Pt 1:12],' will be seen. Who can speak of its beauty,
of its light, of its delight?"[66] But Aelred does indeed speak of that
beauteous, delightful vision:

> The Father will be seen in the Son, the Son in the Father, the
> Holy Spirit in both. He will be seen "not obscurely as in a
> mirror, but face to face [1 Cor 13:12]." For he will be seen
> as he is [see 1 Jn 3:2], fulfilling that promise which says:
> "Those who love me will be loved by my Father, and I shall
> love them and show myself to them [Jn 14:21]." From this
> vision will come knowledge, about which he himself says:
> "This is everlasting life, that they should have knowledge of
> you, the one God, and him whom you have sent, Jesus
> Christ [Jn 17:3]."[67]

Aelred is convinced that the complete fulfillment of the intellect in the
knowledge that comes from heavenly perfection is a source of true
happiness: "... In that perfect vision they enjoy perfect happiness."[68]
The proper response, as Aelred sees it, is rejoicing and praise.[69]

2. The Unity of Love

According to Aelred, knowledge leads to love, both in this life and
after it.[70] The consequences of union with God in love are felt in the
ordering of the will to God and in the victory of the ordered spirit
over the "flesh," one's disordered will.[71] After death and in heaven,
Aelred is sure, "there will be perfect peace, perfect tranquility, for the
flesh will be unable to resist the spirit or the spirit resist God. The
devil will not be able to attack, and neither death nor infirmity will
be able to oppress [the blessed]."[72]

The peace and tranquility that infuse the will perfected in love
are, for Aelred, a participation in the very peace and tranquility that

unite the Trinity.[73] In the life to come, then, the wills of all who have been purged of self-centeredness in this life will be cleansed of all weakness.[74] Thus cleansed, their wills will be filled completely in their new homeland.[75] And this fulfillment will be one of inseparable unity with and in God's love.[76]

3. The Everlasting Memory

Those thus united in love with God are blessed in the afterlife with a memory restored from its beclouded and obscured state.[77] Aelred is confident that, in heaven,

> "my memory lasts for endless generations [Si 24:28]." If you had the remembrance of gold and silver, of riches, how far could this memory extend? Perhaps for many, even a hundred years. For who lives longer than that these days? But if you think of Christ, if you think of Wisdom, the remembrance of these can extend "for endless generations," everlastingly. Wisdom will always exist, and you can always exist with Wisdom, for, as is written, Wisdom is immortal [see Ws 1:15].[78]

As the intellect is perfected in knowledge and the will in love, the perfection of the memory is in a wisdom that lasts forever: ". . . If you think about the kingdom of heaven, of the glory of the angels, of the happiness there is in the vision of God, in incorruption and immortality, this remembrance can extend 'for endless generations [Si 24:28]'—everlastingly, that is—because these things will last forever."[79] The intellect, will, and memory are all filled and fulfilled in the happiness that awaits the pilgrims who journey toward their final home.

4. Joyful Attachment

The *affectus* too will be filled—with great, indeed perfect, joy.[80] It is a joy that will include the perfection of the friendship to which attachment aspires and in which it finds its fulfillment.[81] That friendship is both in and for God—in God when the friendship is for another blessed soul, for God who is the supreme friend.[82]

The joy of friendship will reach its culmination in the communion in God of all the blessed:

> This is that great and wondrous happiness which we await, with God himself acting and diffusing—between himself and the creatures whom he has lifted up, among those degrees and orders which he has differentiated, among the individuals whom he has chosen—so much friendship and true love that each one thus loves the others as herself or himself. By this, just as each one rejoices in his or her own happiness, so does each rejoice in the happiness of the others. Thus the happiness of each belongs to all, and the whole of the happiness of all belongs to each.[83]

All the problems that beset human friendships, from the choice of a friend to the great efforts needed to maintain friendship,[84] are overcome in the community of friends comprising the communion of saints: "There [in heaven], there is no hiding of thoughts, no concealment of affection. This is true and everlasting friendship, which begins in this [life] and is there [in the next] perfected, which here belongs to the few where few are good, but there belongs to all where all are good."[85] Thus, the glories and joys of friendship in this life will be transformed into inexpressible glory and joy in the next.[86]

5. The Glorified Body

The vision, love, and joy that the soul experiences in heaven are not enough for Aelred. To the glories of the soul, he must add those of the body. But for him there is a history that must be acted out and played through in the body's glorification: "We, who have undergone death in body and soul, have the need to rise again in body and in soul. First, however, in the soul, and afterward in the body."[87]

The physical death of the body should bring no fear, Aelred thinks, for "holy and perfected souls enter heaven immediately after this life." "Still," he adds, "their happiness is not complete until they receive their bodies on the day of judgment."[88] They are happy, but "those happy souls wait until the number of their companions is filled up, so that on the day of the [body's] resurrection, clad in the glory of a twofold robe [see Rv 6:11], they may enjoy unending happiness of both body and soul."[89] As Aelred puts it in a sermon for Advent: "By his first coming our Lord raised us up in the soul alone, but by his second coming he will raise us up in the body, so that, as we serve God by both, by the soul and the body, so shall we then possess in both perfect happiness with God."[90]

Thus the resurrection of Jesus will be extended to all happy souls, now reunited with their glorified bodies: "This [Easter] day had a morning, when our Lord was resurrected. It will have a noon, when that glory, that splendor, that brightness, which today begins in the Head, will be poured out on all the parts. Then he will re-fashion 'our lowly body to be like his glorious body [Phil 3:21].'"[91] Consequently, "in paradise the body can be called a body of happiness and of justice,...in that beatitude a body of happiness and of glory."[92] The glorified body will contribute to the beauty of the restored unity of body and soul,[93] and "no trace of diabolic power will remain in the Lord's land, in our flesh, now glorified in an everlasting resurrection."[94]

The resurrected body will "arise with all the perfection and integrity of its nature, but with all its corruption annihilated....Why, then, should we not believe that sensation and motion, having reverted [in death] to those elements from which the body was made, will be taken up again...?"[95] These natural powers will be restored in the body; other powers will be perfected to a preternatural condition: "Then in our bodies will be the perfections of health and beauty, of strength and swiftness...."[96]

As glorious as these gifts are to the body, Aelred concentrates his attention on two others, immortality and incorruption.[97] The liberation of the body from its mortality and corruptibility is, for Aelred, accomplished through the Incarnation of the Son, which itself demonstrates to Aelred the intrinsic value of the human body that now "suffers from corruption, from death, on account of the condemnation for original sin and because of its own self-centeredness and illicit desires....Let us consider that it was so cleansed of the corruption of all its vices and sins that the Son of God himself was born of it and found his rest in it."[98] Those who direct the body lovingly "will have such a reward from our Lord that their bodies will be whole and sound and free of all corruption."[99]

F. The End and Consummation in Happiness

The resurrection of the body at the last judgment will bring, Aelred is sure, a happiness to which humans can look forward with confident hope and expectant joy: "Happy are those who exult in this [Easter] day! Happy are those who possess such a conscience that they not only do not fear the eight days of its octave—for the resurrection of the dead, that is—but rather exult in it!"[100] On that day the contrast between the burdens of this life and the glories of the next will be experienced rather than merely described: "To this life belongs toil, to that life rest. To this life belongs temptation, to that life freedom from care. To this life belongs poverty, to that life riches. To this life belongs struggle, to that life consolation. To this life belong hunger and thirst, to that life satisfaction."[101] The burdens of this life will then be dissolved: "Then will poverty be rewarded with everlasting riches; grief be changed to everlasting joy; for the hungry everlasting satisfaction stored up. No one doubts that all these—riches, joy, satisfaction—are not lacking in happiness."[102] And, Aelred adds: "It is a good thing, brothers, . . . to look forward to a future of everlasting riches, to perpetual delights, to unending joy, to happiness without end."[103]

That future bliss has been prepared as a free gift by the one who was born in Bethlehem, a Bethlehem that can now be built in each human being:

You now build a Bethlehem in your soul, shedding the self-centered love of the world and its riches and false honors. You, yourselves little and humble, see [there] this humble, little boy Jesus. As you gaze on his delightful face, you hear his most pleasant voice: "Come, you blessed of my Father, take possession of the kingdom which has been prepared from the origin of the world [see Mt 25:34]."[104]

The call is inviting; the result of the call's acceptance overwhelming: "Then you will enter that kingdom, and you will see the delightful and lovable Jesus. Then you will be readied and adorned as his bride [see Rv 21:2]; then you will be worthy of his embraces, for you will be without blemish or wrinkle [see Eph 5:27]. Then you will taste the vast array of his sweetnesses [see Ps 30:20] which fill up fully his lovers but which are hidden in this life from the fearful."[105] For Aelred there is nothing more that needs to be said or can be said— save only an exhortation to his hearers to respond lovingly to God's overwhelming love. "Let us pass over," Aelred urges, "pass over by means of hope and longing, by means of love and attachment. 'We see [now] in a mirror but obscurely [1 Cor 13:12],' but, when we have passed over what is imperfect, then we shall see 'face to face [1 Cor 13:12]' that Jesus, our Lord, who lives and reigns with the Father and the Holy Spirit through all ages of ages."[106]

IX

Contemplation

It would seem that the happiness of perfection in this life, and its culmination in the everlasting glories of the next, would be enough for Aelred. And it is. But there is another component of Aelred's spiritual teaching that fits both well and ill his description of the path to perfection. Contemplation is a completely congruent component of Aelred's teaching, but, since it is a component that is not necessary to Aelred's path to the joys of the next world, it seems wise to treat it separately. Since contemplation is an extraordinary phenomenon, it seems wise too to discuss it through illustrations rather than define it at the outset—and this is indeed the way in which Aelred himself approaches the question.

A. The Components of Contemplation

The biblical basis for Aelred's description of contemplation is the account in Second Corinthians of the rapture of Paul: "Carried aloft on the wings of true love, [Paul] penetrates the third heaven [see 2 Cor 12:2]. Tasting in his soul I know not what ineffable [sweetness], he says: 'Eye has not seen or ear heard, it has not occurred to the human heart, what God has prepared for those who love him [1 Cor 2:9; see Is 64:4].'"[1] For Aelred, Paul has clearly experienced something that cannot be described, and so he—and Paul—employ sense imagery to convey something of it—at least of its ineffability. Clearly too Paul's experience is something that he did not initiate; he was "carried aloft." Sometimes Aelred speaks of Paul's passive role in this

120

experience as *raptus fuerit*.[2] The translations could be many: "he was seized"; "he was ravished"; "he was rapt." But all indicate Paul's passivity in the presence of some higher power that is acting.

Paul's experience offers Aelred other elements for his description of contemplation. In a sermon for the feast of Peter and Paul, he comments: "But how this Benjamin [of Gn 49:27] could have been 'in ecstacy of mind [Ps 67:28]' Paul himself discloses when he says of himself: 'I know a man who, fourteen years ago, was caught up into paradise, whether in the body or out of the body I do not know—God knows [2 Cor 12:2].'"[3] Here the active agent is clearly identified as God—which brings no surprise. And, since Paul's body is involved—or, perhaps, left behind—in the experience, Aelred is sure of the obvious: that Paul's experience was in this world and not one experienced in the afterlife. Paul was "caught up"; the Latin is *raptum*. He was "enraptured." This parallels, for Aelred, Benjamin's state "in ecstacy of mind." Rapture and ecstacy are both components of contemplation.

So, Aelred thinks, one can have an experience in this life that God initiates and that involves a degree of ecstacy and rapture such that it cannot be described. Although in this life and thus in the body, such an experience does not involve the bodily senses: "...As long as humans live in the body, they are influenced by the bodily senses; during their waking hours they are rarely detached from them, as when, for example, they are carried off in rapture."[4] "Carried off in rapture" could also be translated "rapt in ecstacy."[5]

Because the rapturous, ecstatic experience of contemplation is ineffable, Aelred resorts to poetic imagery to describe it. One such image is intoxication: "He [Paul] himself was caught up *[raptus]* in contemplation, 'up to the third heaven [2 Cor 12:2],' and was intoxicated with that wine which is wont to gladden 'the heart of humans [Ps 103:15].'"[6] Aelred explains his image in a sermon on the Epiphany of the Lord:

Some intoxication is physical, some is spiritual. There is physical intoxication when one loses or confuses one's own sense or reason through excessive drink. Spiritual intoxication, however, is sometimes good, sometimes bad. Bad when, through some sort of excess or self-centeredness, one fails to serve the ends of justice and reason. Good when, through revelation or contemplation or great love, one rises above human reason and sense and is intoxicated "with the richness of the house" of God and made drunk from its "torrent of pleasure [Ps 35:9]." In describing this intoxication the apostle says: "When we rise above our mind, it is to God; when we are sober, it is for you [2 Cor 5:13]."[7]

Contemplation is not irrational; it is super-rational. But is it not the same as revelation.

If intoxication is an appropriate image for the contemplative experience, the image of sexual union offers Aelred a still more useful image:

These are the secrets of the Bridegroom and the bride [in their embrace]. These are their extraordinary delights, in which no one else shares. "My secret is my own; my secret is my own [Is 24:16]." In what is your secret, O bride? You alone experience the delights of him when, in a spiritual kiss, created and uncreated spirits join and are merged so that two become one. I do indeed say "one," as justifying and justified, as sanctifying and sanctified, as deifying and deified.[8]

The contemplative experience is not only initiated by God, it is an experience of God.

But, if contemplative union is initiated and consummated by God, the human soul has a part to play as well. She must prepare her bridal bed with virtues that will attract him, as Aelred relates in another image, this time an agricultural one:

If we should wish, my brothers, to have this [second] Adam [Jesus Christ] dwell in our heart, we must there prepare a paradise for him. May the soil of our heart be fertile and fecund, abounding in virtues like spiritual trees. May the Spirit be there, like a never-failing fountain which irrigates us

> spiritually with grace, compunction, devotion, and all sorts
> of spiritual delight. May the four virtues be there, like four
> rivers which wash us clean of all the grime of vice and render
> us unsullied and unstained. All this so that we may be fit for
> the Lord's embrace![9]

And the best preparation for the Bridegroom's loving embrace is a
heart itself filled with love: "This is the abundance of your house, in
which your lovers become so inebriated [see Ps 35:9] that, quitting
themselves, they pass into you—how else, Lord, save by loving you."[10]

The preparation for contemplation is the same path of virtue, the
same way of love, that pilgrim souls must take in preparing for perfection. So Aelred expects those who aspire to perfection to make themselves ready for contemplation; "thus beginners aim at virtue, those
progressing at true humility, the perfect at contemplation . . . ."[11]

Aelred's model for contemplation is the virgin Mary, presented
in the temple by her parents: "She enters 'into the sanctuary of God,'
who pours out his life on her. And so she passes over 'to the place of
the wondrous tabernacle, up to the abode of God [see Ps 41:5].' She
is caught up *[rapitur]* by some power of contemplation to 'the judgment seat of Christ [2 Cor 5:10],' and she sees the invisible and
hears the ineffable."[12] Aelred is here celebrating Mary's presentation
on earth, not her assumption into heaven. Contemplation is not
beatific vision.

B. WHAT CONTEMPLATION IS NOT

Although contemplation—in the sense that Aelred has been describing it—is not the vision of God seen in heaven, Aelred often uses the
word *contemplatio,* and its verbal form *contemplare,* to describe the
intellectual perfection that comes in the next life. The difficulty is,
then, in attempting to ascertain that state, terrestrial and temporary
or celestial and everlasting, to which Aelred refers in any particular
passage that employs these words. When Aelred indicates that the
contemplative experience is temporary, then one can be sure that he

means a contemplation experienced in this life, "for contemplation
. . . cannot be continual in this life . . . ."[13]

Sometimes it is quite clear that Aelred is referring to the beatific
vision, even when he uses the word *contemplatio*. For example, when,
in his *Mirror of Love,* he affirms that "in contemplation of the divine
light all the darkness of error is dispersed . . . ,"[14] the context clearly
establishes that Aelred means to indicate the beatific vision, to which
"kingdom of tranquility true and perfect love has transported its
followers . . . ."[15] Sometimes the context conveys insufficient information to ascertain whether Aelred is speaking of contemplation or using
"contemplation" to indicate the beatific vision. Thus, Aelred speaks,
in his *Twenty-ninth Sermon on the Burdens of Isaiah,* of souls, "like
fledglings flying from the nest."[16] Then he adds: "By this we understand . . . the flight which reaches the perfection of contemplation."[17]
It is difficult to determine from the context whether the destination is
terrestrial or celestial.[18] But, whether Aelred's use of the word "contemplation" pertains to heavenly vision or the contemplation experienced on the path to heaven, it is clear that he distinguishes the two.

A similar difficulty emerges in Aelred's frequent use of "contemplation" to indicate meditation, an intense activity of the intellect
aimed at understanding the truth about oneself, the world around
one, and the Creator of both.[19] However graced or inspired by God,[20]
meditation involves intellectual action, not the passive, though ecstatic, reception of the gift of contemplation.[21]

For example, intellectual activity is clearly indicated in Aelred's
injunction to "contemplate" in *On Reclusion:* " . . . Do you not think
you will gain some delight for yourself if you contemplate *[contem-
pleris]* him [Jesus] at Nazareth as a boy among boys, if you behold
him obedient to his mother and assisting his foster-father with his
work?"[22] The parallel between "contemplate" and "behold" makes
Aelred's meaning clear. Then too, the joining of "contemplation" to
"love" in one of Aelred's Advent sermons—"the creature is perfected
by contemplation and love of God . . ."[23]—indicates the fulfillment of
the faculties of intellect and will, and not an ecstatic experience. On
occasion, Aelred equates "contemplation" and "good thoughts,"[24]
and sometimes he uses "contemplate" to indicate simply "behold."[25]

But it is also true that Aelred sometimes uses "contemplation" to indicate an exalted state of meditation. In such cases his language and imagery can make the meditative state sound much like contemplation. For example, in speaking of stability, silence, and solitude in a sermon on John the Baptizer, Aelred says: "There are three things which impede this solitude: wandering, distrust, curiosity. Those who can protect themselves against these three ... are to sit and be silent and raise themselves above themselves [see Lam 3:28]. This sitting signifies stability; this silence signifies quiet; this raising signifies the sublimity of contemplation."[26] Being raised above oneself in contemplation surely sounds like a rapturous experience, but Aelred goes on to say:

> These three [stability, quiet, and contemplation] can be possessed by those who can avoid those three impediments which I have mentioned. For those who wander are surely not able to sit; those who are distrustful surely cannot remain silent; those too who are curious cannot grasp that their heart is alone. These are the dying flies of which the prophet says: "Dying flies spoil the sweetness of the oil [Qo 10:1]." The oil is a spiritual anointing in the love and contemplation of God.[27]

The virtues which "can be possessed" are not the contemplative state in which one is possessed. The juxtaposition of love and contemplation once more indicates the fulfillment of the faculties, and thus "contemplation" becomes here another word for "knowledge."

Aelred's clear distinction between meditation and contemplation may sometimes seem so blurred by his language as to be misleading. This is surely the case in Aelred's treatise *On Reclusion,* where he says:

> How often has he [God] stood at your side because you were fainting with fear? How often has he poured himself into your inmost being because you were burning with love? How often has he explained the spiritual sense when you were singing psalms or reading? How often has he swept you

away *[rapiebat]* with some ineffable longing while you were
at prayer? How often has he transported your soul, with-
drawn from earthly things, to heavenly delights and the pleasures of paradise?[28]

Rapiebat might well be translated "rapt" or "ravished," and seems to
indicate contemplative ecstasy. But caution is indicated when one
considers that Aelred's use of *raptus* elsewhere does not always indicate that he is speaking of contemplation[29] and that he sometimes
uses intensely sexual imagery to describe spiritual practices that could
not be called contemplation.[30] The fear, love, psalm singing, and
reading to which Aelred here refers are conditions or activities of the
soul in search of God, not the possession of him; Jesus' explanation
of the spiritual sense of a scriptural passage is grace-filled enlighten-
ment, not ecstasy. And the recluse is "swept away" with longing, not
fulfillment.[31]

Though meditation is not contemplation,[32] Aelred teaches that it
can lead to the contemplative experience. In a sermon on the Annunciation, Aelred employs sensual and sexual imagery to illustrate the
contemplative experience for which the soul longs:

Happy are those who open the door of their hearts to you,
good Jesus! You will enter it so that there you may feed,
there you may rest at midday [see Sg 1:6]. Your coming,
Lord, brings the noon of heavenly light to the chaste heart,
calming every emotion of the heart with an infusion of
divine peace. You strew the most delightful bed on which
you lie with a most appealing covering of spiritual flowers
and scents, so that then the soul, from her perception of you
and from the unexpected sweetness of her delight at that
stillness, bursts forth, with wondrous affection, into a cry of
exultation and acknowledgment: "You are fair, my beloved,
and comely. Our bed is covered with flowers [Sg 1:15]."[33]

Aelred then shifts from the imagery of the bridal bed to an image of
nourishment, signaling a shift from contemplation to the consideration or meditation that often precedes it: "Of what is this banquet

prepared? Of butter and honey [see Is 7:15]. O Lord, on what do you feed in us save our soul's devotion? This devotion is a sort of delightful attachment [arising] from a twofold consideration of the humanity and, it is clear, the divinity of Christ."[34] This meditation, this consideration, can prepare the soul for an ecstatic experience, if the Lord will but take her to himself:

> Ravished [rapta] out of her senses by heavenly delights, she beholds the glory of her Creator and is delighted by the splendor of his beautiful face. Through her ardor of unutterable joy and her delight in inexpressible affection, she crosses over completely into God. There, filled with the sweetness of heavenly honey, she tastes and sees how sweet is the Lord [see Ps 33:9], how blessed are all who hope in him [see Ps 83:13]....[35]

Aelred returns to the soul, ardently longing for such an experience, to counsel her to meditation: "So when the soul is longing and hungering and sighing for the things of heaven, the water from the sublime spring of heavenly wisdom will flow into her with its sweetness of intimate affection, and this heavenly dew will be changed into honey."[36] Meditation is a preparation for union with God; contemplation is the terrestrial consummation of that union.

But contemplation is not a vision; it has nothing to do with dreams; it is much more than spiritual visitation or consolation. In Aelred's *Third Sermon on the Burdens of Isaiah,* he tells the story of a nun who saw a vision of Christ "hanging from the cross, fastened with nails, pierced by a lance, with his blood flowing out through five openings...."[37] Aelred comments: "Whatever can be determined about visions other [than those of the prophets] is uncertain, and is confirmed more by faith than by science."[38] In Aelred's treatise *On the Soul,* after describing at some length a series of visions and dreams drawn from the Old Testament,[39] he declares: "These sorts of dreams must not be given easy credence....I have said...that some people are punished by dreams and others are corrected. To this I would add that some are instructed and others deceived, some are entangled in error and others purged [of it]."[40] Visions and dreams are, for Aelred, at best a mixed bag, quite unlike the glorious and indescribable experience of contemplation.

Aelred is not ambiguous about another sort of spiritual phenomenon: "These are the spiritual visitations and consolations by which we are delighted for now,... until we arrive at our perfect inheritance."[41] But, as positively as Aelred speaks of these visitations of the Spirit,[42] they are not all contemplative in character.

C. THE THIRD VISITATION

The middle and largest part of Book 2 of Aelred's *The Mirror of Love* is ostensibly a treatise on compunction. But it is much more.[43] It is a description of three stages in the spiritual life, centering on the image of the soul's three visitations by God and the consolations given in each visitation:

> The reason for this [sort of] visitation is threefold. It sometimes serves to arouse, it sometimes serves to console, and it even serves as a great reward. To arouse those sleeping, to console those toiling, as a reward for those sighing for celestial things. So the first arouses the sluggish; the second refreshes those toiling; the third lifts up those ascending. The first compunction rouses to holiness; the second safeguards holiness; the third rewards. The first frightens the disdainful or entices the fearful; the second supports and advances those striving to flourish; the third embraces those arriving. The first is like a goad correcting those straying; the second is like a staff supporting the weak; the third is a bed supporting the resting.[44]

It is the third visitation that is most important here.

Each visitation is a gift, of course—a gift unmerited, in its first two forms, by the holiness of the recipient.[45] But Aelred seems to suggest that the third visitation is the reward of the virtuous: "When one has become accustomed to frequent compunction in the second sort [of visitation], nourished often by little droughts of divine sweetness, one is exalted to that more sublime, more excellent level [of visitation], which no longer sustains the weak but rewards the near-perfect with more abundant grace."[46] There is a pelagian—or semi-pelagian—ring to this statement that accords badly with Aelred's description of contemplation accomplished "through the Spirit of God, by the infusion of grace."[47] Aelred rather self-consciously corrects any possible confusion: "Therefore, just as in that [first] state [God's] loving-kindness operates alone, without preceding merit, so too in this [third] state, justice functions with mercy in crowning his [God's] gifts—gifts which he has, nonetheless, willed to be our merits."[48] Orthodoxy is affirmed; the third visitation is a gift: "Admitted by the grace of divine kindness to that most sublime sort of consolation, which is, as it were, the reward of the just, you will say with the prophet: 'How great is the abundance of your delight, O Lord, which you have hidden away for those who stand in awe of you [Ps 30:20].'"[49] Aelred caps his insistence on the primacy of grace by adding: "...[And so] in the third [visitation]...'let anyone who boasts, boast in the Lord [2 Cor 10:17].'"[50]

Aelred's description of this third visitation employs rich sensual imagery and includes the word "contemplation":[51]

> In this state, the soul, accustomed to the countless incitements of heavenly attachments, is exalted by degrees to that most sublime sort of visitation experienced by very few. There one begins to enjoy some foretaste of the first-fruits of one's future rewards. Passing into the awe-inspiring tabernacle, right up to the dwelling-place of God [see Ps 41:5], with soul melting within, one is inebriated with the nectar of celestial secrets. Contemplating with the purest of gazes the place of one's future rest, one cries out with the prophet: "This is my resting place for ages of ages; here shall I dwell, for I have chosen it [Ps 131:14]."[52]

Contemplation is thus a rapturous foretaste of celestial bliss.

Aelred expresses his longing for that ecstatic experience in language charged with sexual imagery: "...Burning for the hotly-desired embraces of him who is 'the fairest of all humankind's sons

[Ps 44:3],' [the soul] begins to desire 'to be dissolved and to be with Christ [Phil 1:23],' saying each day with the prophet: 'Woe is me that my sojourn has been prolonged [Ps 119:5].'"53 Aelred sees that longing fulfilled as favored souls are "cherished in the most delightful and purest embraces of Jesus."54

The rewards of the contemplative embrace are many and glorious:

> ...As you enter the glory of God, flaming with the unsullied ardor of true love, you will be happily satiated, as if by the fruit of the promised land. As the fire of divine love completely consumes the yoke of self-centeredness, you will rest in the mellow glow of gold, in the splendor of wisdom, in the delight of divine contemplation. And you will experience fully that the yoke of the Lord is delightful and his burden light [see Mt 11:30].55

Aelred's anticipation of these rewards is infectious: "... In the third [visitation] 'true and perfect love casts out all fear [1 Jn 4:18].'"56 In contemplation he finds that which all seek: "The fruit of the third [visitation] is perfect happiness,... delightful devotion toward God."57 He proclaims to all how "it is delightful and secure restoration for those standing at the summit of perfection."58 In the mouth of the novice to whom this good news is proclaimed, Aelred puts what he thinks is the proper response: "... I am confident that someday I shall attain that sublime and ineffable [state]."59

D. THE SABBATH OF SABBATHS

In that contemplative state the soul rests on the sabbath of sabbaths, which is Aelred's vehicle for describing contemplation in Book 3 of his *Mirror of Love*.60 Sometimes Aelred speaks in that book, in exalted language, of the beatific vision.61 But he uses the phrase "sabbath of sabbaths" to point to its anticipation in this world in contemplation: "Meanwhile, you have ... the sabbath of sabbaths, as a sort of foretaste."62

All three of Aelred's sabbaths are expressions of love:

> ... Let the first sabbath [of days] represent one's love of self,
> the second [the sabbath of years] love of neighbor, the sab-
> bath of sabbaths the love of God....The [third, the] spiri-
> tual sabbath, is rest for the spirit, peace of heart, tranquility
> of mind. This sabbath is sometimes experienced in love of
> self, at other times it is drawn from delight in love for others,
> and, beyond all doubt, it is brought to perfection in love of
> God.[63]

This last statement might seem to deny that Aelred's sabbath of sabbaths is truly contemplation, but Aelred explains that love of self and
of neighbor are necessary prerequisites to the all-consuming love
experienced in contemplation:

> The greater the soul's devotion, the more surely does she,
> truly purified by the twin loves [of self and neighbor], long
> for the blissful embraces of his [the Lord's] divinity. So that,
> inflamed with the most ardent desire, she rises above the veil
> of the flesh and, entering into that sanctuary where Christ
> Jesus is the breath on her face [see Lam 4:20], she is thor-
> oughly absorbed by that ineffable light, by that extraordinary
> delight.[64]

In that light and delight, Aelred teaches, "all that is corporeal, all
that is sensible, all that is mutable, is reduced to silence. She [the
soul] fixes her clear-sighted gaze on what is and is so always and is in
itself: on the One. She is free to see that the Lord himself is God. In
the tender embrace of True Love himself she keeps a sabbath which
is undoubtedly the sabbath of sabbaths."[65]

In the contemplative experience the intellect is fulfilled in the
vision of Truth itself. The will too is fulfilled in embracing him who
is Love. And the *affectus* is filled with blissful delight. "This," Aelred
says, "is the jubilee year, in which humans 'return to their possession
[Lv 25:10],' to their very Author, so that they may truly be possessed [by him] and possess [him], be had [by him] and have [him],

be held [by him] and hold [him]. . . . On this sabbath all servile fear is cast out, self-centered desires of the body—even the memory of them—are lulled to sleep, and the fullness of the Spirit is received."[66] In contemplation, the body and the memory join the intellect, will, and *affectus* in fulfillment. The sabbath of sabbaths also completes the effects of the preceding two sabbaths:

> On the first sabbath [the soul] is freed of fault, on the second
> of self-centeredness, on the third of absolutely everything that
> distracts her. On the first the soul tastes how sweet is Jesus in
> his humanity; on the second she sees how perfect he is in true
> love; on the third she sees how sublime he is in [his] divine
> nature. On the first she is re-collected within herself, on the
> second she is extended outside herself, and on the third she is
> seized and carried off *[raptitur]* above herself.[67]

Near the end of Book 3 of Aelred's *Mirror of Love*, he describes the rapture of the apostle Paul in a way that convinces one that Aelred is speaking too of his own experience:

> . . . He says: "I have chosen to be separated from Christ for
> my sisters and brothers [Rom 9:3]." This can be understood,
> not inappropriately, [to mean] that—from that hidden prayer
> in which he rested delightfully in the embrace of Jesus, from
> that ineffable height of contemplation in which he surveyed,
> with the purest of eyes, the secrets of the heavenly mysteries,
> from the delight of that purest compunction which bathed
> with the sweetest dew of spiritual attachment that soul thirst-
> ing for the things of heaven—he would have chosen to be
> called forth into the din of the world for the sake of the salva-
> tion of his sisters and brothers. None who, in their own way,
> are free to taste how sweet is the Lord [see Ps 33:9] and how
> blessed are they who hope in him [see Ps 39:5] could doubt
> that this calling forth must be called separation from Christ.[68]

Here Aelred introduces a new component of contemplation. The contemplative, readied for rapture by love of self and of neighbor, must leave his or her exalted state of love for God to return to the world left behind. The return too must be loving: the neighbor's welfare cries out for, demands, this sacrifice.

E. The Fulfillment of Friendship

For Aelred there is thus a necessary link between contemplation and love of neighbor. There is also a close bond between contemplation and that special relationship with others called "friendship." Spiritual friendship is expressed through a spiritual kiss, a kiss in which the Spirit of God participates:

> ...A spiritual kiss is properly the kiss of friends who are bound by the one law of friendship. It is not made by the touching of the mouth but by the attachment of the soul, not by the union of the lips but by the mingling of spirits. All this is purified by the Spirit of God, and, through his participation, it gives off a celestial savor. I would call this, not inappropriately [I think], the kiss of Christ. Yet he himself does not offer it from his own mouth but by that of another, inspiring in the lovers his most holy attachment so that it seems to them they are like one soul in separate bodies. And [thus] they may say with the prophet: "See how good and how pleasing it is for brothers to dwell together in unity [Ps 132:1]."[69]

Thus spiritual friendship becomes a preparation for the ecstatic experience of God: "...The soul, accustomed to the [spiritual] kiss [of friendship]...delights solely in the kiss of Christ and rests in his embrace."[70] So, for Aelred, the union of friends can lead to the delights of rapturous contemplation: "Such a reward there then will be for those cultivating it [friendship], when, totally transported into God, it immerses in contemplation of him those whom it has united."[71]

But the obligations of love are also the obligations of friendship: the contemplative must return from the ecstatic experience of God to

his neighbor, now his friend. In *On Spiritual Friendship,* love's obligation becomes a joy—a joy expressed in Aelred's eulogy of his sub-
prior Simon: "Was it not a sharing in beatitude thus to love and be
loved, so to help and be helped, and thus to fly up ever higher from
the delights of fraternal and true love to that still more sublime and
splendid height of divine love? To mount up, by the ladder of true
love, to the embrace of Christ himself, then to descend to love of my
neighbor, there pleasantly to rest?"[72]

F. THE END OF THE JOURNEY

In his *On Jesus at the Age of Twelve,* Aelred describes this motion of
the soul not as an ascent but as a journey. It is a journey with Jesus
from Bethlehem to Nazareth to Jerusalem: "As Bethlehem, where
Christ was born little and poor, is the beginning of the good life, as
Nazareth, where he was brought up, is the practice of the virtues, so
Jerusalem, to which he went up at the age of twelve, is the contemplation of the celestial secrets."[73] The soul's journey takes her "from
the valley of tears, along the rough road of temptation, through the
broad expanse of spiritual practices, to the height of luminous contemplation."[74]

There the soul joins the twelve-year-old Jesus, who has come to
Jerusalem, and there she too enters the twelfth year of her spiritual
life, the year "of contemplation. This raises up the ardent soul to the
heavenly Jerusalem itself. It unlocks heaven and opens the gates of
paradise. It reveals to her, contemplating with the eyes of a pure
mind, the Bridegroom himself, more beautiful than the other children of God [see Ps 44:3], 'looking out through the lattice-work
[Sg 2:9]'...."[75] What Christ sees through the lattice-work is the
approach of his love, an approach made possible by her growth in
virtue: "Having been cleansed of the defilement of the passions, she
flies up from the snares which have trapped her. The memory of her
past has been obliterated, and the images of the external have vanished. With the most vehement desire, she raises up the fair face of
her heart to discern him whom she loves. And so she is worthy to
hear: 'You are totally beautiful'...."[76] The soul's perfection in virtue

signals a change of seasons: "'The winter,' he says, 'is past; the rain is over and gone. The flowers have appeared [Sg 2:11–12].' These flowers so fresh are the virtues, which spring up happily in the field of the heart of her [who is] progressing so well after the trials of winter and the rains of temptation."[77] Christ, thus allured by the attractions of the virtuous soul, takes her to himself as a beautiful bride: "Then there are kisses, then embraces.... Then my soul abounds in delights, enjoys good things, and celebrates in Jerusalem a feast day with exultation and joy."[78] Jesus' bride is delirious with joy, then aghast that their union is so brief: "But alas, alas, how rare the moment and how short the stay!"[79]

Despite the transitory nature of the contemplative experience, Aelred is confident that some, if not all, of his audience will enjoy such rapture—if they are only open to it through the practice of virtue:

> If, at the end [of your meditations], all those [mundane] matters, regardless of how great, how splendid, or how sublime, seem of little account—such is your longing for one kiss, for one touch of his delightful lips. If you begin to cry out with a plaintive voice with the prophet: "I have sought your face; your face, Lord, I seek again [Ps 26:8]." If you cry out: "Who will give me you for my brother, nursed at the breasts of my mother, that I might meet you outside and kiss you [Sg 8:1]?," then surely he will come to you, in the fragrance of ointments and spices [see Sg 1:3 and 5:1]. Pressing on your soul some heavenly and divine kiss, he will fill your inmost being with celestial and ineffable delight, so that you will joyfully cry out: "Grace has been poured forth from your lips [Ps 44:3]!"[80]

G. WAS AELRED A CONTEMPLATIVE?

In view of what has been heard from Aelred on the matter of contemplation, the question seems impertinent. His descriptions of the contemplative experience ring true with the sound of his own experience.

But why then does he say, in the midst of one such description: "Would that I too might sense how great is the multitude of those delights which he stores up for those who stand in awe of him [see Ps 30:20]"?[81]

I think the answer lies in Aelred's magisterial role as abbot. As we have seen, Aelred sees his audience as composed of many and diverse sorts of souls: those setting out the spiritual journey, those progressing on it, and those perfected as much as is possible in this life.[82] Among them are novices whom Aelred would excite to emulation of his longing for the contemplative experience.[83] Aelred's cry of unfulfilled longing is, I think, evidence of a rhetorical humility through which he seeks to identify with those in his audience taking the first steps on the path to perfection.[84]

Aelred's role as a teacher of contemplation leads him to describe the rapture of Paul.[85] It also leads him to tell his hearers a story about a nun he knows:

> One day it happened that, when she was devoting herself with love to private prayer, a sort of wondrous delight came over her, driving out all her mental functions, all her thought processes, and, what is more, all the spiritual attachment she had for her friends. Her soul was then rapt *[rapitur]* up above herself, as if bidding farewell to all the world's burdens. Caught up by some ineffable and incomprehensible light, . . . she began to know Christ himself—not as before, according to the flesh—but now not according to the flesh [see 2 Cor 5:16], for the Spirit had led her before the true face of Christ Jesus, as he is in himself.[86]

Since the nun's experience was as ineffable as Paul's, there is no way that Aelred can know that her experience was truly contemplative. But it is clear that Aelred believes in the genuineness of her experience.

It is likewise impossible for anyone to know with certainty that Aelred's own experience is a contemplative rapture initiated by God. It is clear, however, that Aelred's biographer, Walter Daniel, believes Aelred had such an ecstatic experience. Walter relates:

> In all the various events which follow, I myself took part. I
> make an exception in that I did not see him rapt—"in the
> body or out of the body I do not know; God knows [2 Cor
> 12:2]"—up to indescribable visions flowing with honey. But
> he told me privately that he himself had experienced such
> sights. [He reported that], in comparison with his delight in
> them, whatever delights which came from the flesh were
> entirely forgotten and [that] he was completely unaware of
> any temporal concerns—if any had been present.[87]

And we too, though we can not be sure of the nature of Aelred's
experience, can confidently assert that he had *some* sort of extraordinary experience and that he believed he was united with God in it.
Otherwise, how could he have written: "...If the soul is not only
tamed in its terrestrial attachments, but even its wandering is brought
to rest, it will transcend all that is terrestrial—all that is invisible, imag-
inary, and everything else besides. Thus departing the world, the dead
live in God, entering the third heaven and walking in the secret places
of paradise [see Gn 3:8]."[88] The "dead" here are those who have died
for a time to the cares of the world through contemplation, but then
are "recalled to corporeal attachments."[89] Aelred reports that, despite
its brevity, "this [experience] is total perfection."[90] Whether or not
one believes Aelred is truly what he claims to be, a contemplative, it is
surely clear that his understanding of the path to perfect happiness is a
many-faceted and sophisticated vision. It is likewise clear—at least to
me—that he is a splendid teacher of that path.

Notes

1. An Introduction to Aelred

1. The material in this short sketch has been drawn from the following sources: Émile Brouette, "Aelred de Rievaulx," in *Dictionnaire des Auteurs Cisterciens,* Documentation Cistercienne 16 (Rochefort, Belgique: Abbaye Notre Dame de Rochefort, 7 vols., 1975–1979) 1:10–17; Charles Dumont, "Aelred of Rievaulx: His Life and Works," the introduction to Aelred of Rievaulx, *The Mirror of Charity,* trans. Elizabeth Connor; CF 17 (Kalamazoo, Michigan: Cistercian Publications, 1990), pp. 11–67; Marsha Dutton, "Introduction to Walter Daniel's *Vita Aelredi,*" in Walter Daniel, *The Life of Aelred of Rievaulx,* CF 57 (Kalamazoo, Michigan; Spencer, Massachusetts: Cistercian Publications, 1994), pp. 7–46; David Knowles, *The Monastic Order in England: A History of Its Development from the Times of St Dunstan to the Fourth Lateran Council, 943–1216* (Cambridge: Cambridge University Press, 1950), pp. 241–45, 255, and 257–66; F. M. Powicke, "Introduction" to *Vita Aelredi Abbatis Rievall'* (London, Edinburgh, Paris, Melbourne, Toronto, New York: Thomas Nelson and Sons Ltd, 1950, reprinted 1963), pp. ix–lxxxix; Douglas Roby, "Introduction" to Aelred of Rievaulx, *Spiritual Friendship,* CF 5 (Washington, DC: Cistercian Publications, 1974), pp. 3–14; and Aelred Squire, *Aelred of Rievaulx: A Study,* CS 50 (Kalamazoo, Michigan: Cistercian Publications, 1981; a reprint of London: S.P.C.K., 1969), pp. 1–50. Thomas Merton's "St Aelred and the Cistercians" (edited by Patrick Hart in CSQ 20 [1985] 212–25; 21 [1986] 30–42; 22 [1987] 55–75; 23 [1988] 45–62; 24 [1989] 50–68) contains many details of Aelred's life, charmingly told.

2. Aelred's title and duties at the Scottish court have been described variously. See Roby, "Introduction," p. 6; Powicke, "Introduction," pp. xl–xli; and Dutton, "Introduction," p. 24.

3. Marsha Dutton thinks that Aelred had planned the visit and that that was part of his motivation in accepting David's commission. See Dutton, "Introduction," p. 26. Elsewhere she has written: "Surely Aelred left the court and journeyed to Yorkshire precisely to enter into monastic life, to turn from the world of the court to that of the cloister, not through sudden impulse or previously unheard divine summons, but through careful, studied decision." Dutton, "The Conversion and Vocation of Aelred of Rievaulx: A Historical Hypothesis," in Daniel Williams, ed., *England in the Twelfth Century: Proceedings of the 1988 Harlaxton Symposium* (n.p.: The Boydall Press, 1990), p. 44.

4. Bernard's letter has been edited in CCCM 1:3–4 and SBOp 8:486–89. The letter appears in English as part of Elizabeth Connor's translation of *The Mirror of Charity*, CF 17:69–72.

5. Aelred seems to indicate that, at one point, presumably just before or during the first years of his abbacy, his community numbered three hundred. See Spec car 2.17.43; CCCM 1:87; CF 17:195.

6. Walter Daniel, Aelred's biographer, asserts that, at Aelred's death, there were 640 monks living at Rievaulx. See *Vita Ailredi Abbatis Rievall'*, ed. F. M. Powicke with a facing English translation (London, Edinburgh, Paris, Melbourne, Toronto, New York: Thomas Nelson and Sons Ltd, 1950, reprinted 1963), p. 38 (p. 119 in the reprinted translation in CF 57).

7. The extent to which the abbot of Rievaulx was burdened by concern for temporal matters is well illustrated in an article by Janet Burton, "The Estates and Economy of Rievaulx Abbey in Yorkshire," Cîteaux 49 (1998) 29–94. For Aelred specifically, see pp. 33–37.

8. Knowles estimates that the journey to the Chapter General and the visitations consumed some three to four months of Aelred's year. See *Monastic Order*, p. 263.

9. These activities are chronicled in some detail in Douglas Roby's "Chimaera of the North: The Active Life of Aelred of Rievaulx," in John R. Sommerfeldt, ed., *Cistercian Ideals and Reality*, CS 60 (Kalamazoo, Michigan: Cistercian Publications, 1978), pp. 152–69.

10. See Knowles, *Monastic Order*, p. 240.

11. Virtually all (some three hundred) of Aelred's letters were lost in the sixteenth century. See Roby, "Chimaera," in *Cistercian Ideals and Reality*, p. 152.

12. Dutton, "Introduction," p. 41.

13. Aelred's motivation in writing this work is discussed by Aelred

Glidden in his "Aelred the Historian: The Account of the Battle of the Standard," in John R. Sommerfeldt, ed., *Erudition at God's Service: Studies in Medieval Cistercian History, XI,* CS 98 (Kalamazoo, Michigan: Cistercian Publications Inc., 1987), pp. 175–84.

14. See Louis J. Lekai, *The Cistercians: Ideals and Reality* (Kent, Ohio: The Kent State University Press, 1977), p. 366. This splendid book is an excellent source of information on Cistercian life in all its many facets.

15. *Aelredi Rievallensis Sermones I–XLVI,* CCCM 2A, and *Sermones XLVII–LXXXIV,* CCCM 2B.

16. *Sermones inediti b. Aelredi abbatis Rievallensis,* Series Scriptorum S. Ordinis Cisterciensis I (Rome: apud Curiam Generalem Sacri Ordinis Cisterciensis, 1952). Now superseded by CCCM 2B.

17. Walter Daniel, *Vita Aelredi* 31; Powicke, p. 40; CF 57:120.

18. Walter Daniel, *Vita Aelredi* 51; Powicke, p. 58; CF 57:135.

19. Dutton, "Conversion," in *England in the Twelfth Century,* p. 31.

20. I do not intend to offer a bibliographical essay here. The bibliographies that are most useful are: Anselm Hoste, *Bibliotheca Aelrediana: A Survey of the Manuscripts, Old Catalogues, Editions and Studies Concerning St. Aelred of Rievaulx,* Instrumenta Patristica II (Steenbrugis: in Abbatia Sancti Petri; Hagae Comitis: Martinus Nijhoff, 1962); and Pierre-André Burton, *Bibliotheca Aelrediana secunda: Une bibliographie cumulative (1962–1996),* Fédération Internationale des Instituts d'Études Médiévales, Textes et Études du Moyen Âge, 7 (Louvain-la-Neuve: n.p., 1997).

21. The names that demand inclusion in any list of monastic contributors to Aelredian studies are those of Odo Brooke, Anselm Hoste, Anselme LeBail, Gaetano Raciti, Robert Thomas, and André Wilmart. Their contributions can be found in the bibliographies, noted above, by Hoste and Burton.

22. Paris: J. Galbalda et Cie, 1959.

23. Translated by Columban Heaney in CS 2 (Shannon, Ireland: Irish University Press, 1962).

24. *La Spiritualité de Cîteaux* (Paris: au Portulan chez Flammarion, 1955). Translated by Elizabeth A. Livingstone as *The Cistercian Heritage* (London: A. R. Mowbray & Co. Limited, 1958).

25. See Powicke, "Introduction," pp. ix–cii.

26. Powicke was co-editor, with Anselm Hoste, of the critical edition of Aelred's treatises (CCCM 1) and editor of one of the collections of Aelred's sermons (see above, n. 16).

27. London: S.P.C.K., 1969.

28. CS 50 (Kalamazoo, Michigan: Cistercian Publications, 1981).

29. See Columban Heaney, "Aelred of Rievaulx: His Relevance to the Post Vatican II Age," in M. Basil Pennington, ed., *The Cistercian Spirit: A Symposium in Memory of Thomas Merton,* CS 3 (Spencer, Massachusetts: Cistercian Publications, 1970), pp. 166–89.

30. Vatican II, *Perfectae caritatis* (28 October 1965) 2; trans. in Austin Flannery, ed., *Vatican Council II: The Conciliar and Post Conciliar Documents* (Collegeville, Minnesota: Liturgical Press, 1975), p. 612.

31. Bede Jarrett, "St. Aelred of Rievaulx (1110–1166)," in Maisie Ward, ed., *The English Way* (New York: Sheed and Ward, 1933), p. 87.

32. Bernard McGinn, *The Growth of Mysticism,* The Presence of God: A History of Western Christian Mysticism II (New York: Crossroad, 1994), p. 323.

33. In Cîteaux 13 (1962) 5–17, 97–132.

34. Cuernavaca, Mexico: Centro Intercultural de Documentacion, 1970. Aelred is discussed on pp. 18/1–49.

35. In *Cistercian Ideals and Reality,* pp. 187–98.

36. In Coll 51 (1989) 78–88.

37. See Burton, *Bibliotheca . . . secunda,* pp. 131–33.

38. Burton, *Bibliotheca . . . secunda,* pp. 133–35.

39. Chicago: University of Chicago Press, 1980. Boswell's thesis has been questioned by, among others, Glenn W. Olsen in "The Gay Middle Ages: A Response to Professor Boswell," *Communio: International Catholic Review* 8 (1981) 119–38; and J. Robert Wright, "Boswell on Homosexuality: A Case Undemonstrated," *Anglican Theological Review* 66 (1984) 79–84.

40. New York: Crossroad, 1994.

41. Among these reviews are some that are favorable; for example: Thomas H. Bestul, in *Speculum* 71 (1996) 465–67; and Arjo Vanderjagt, in CSQ 31 (1996) 225–26. Among those reviews that show dissatisfaction with McGuire's book are: Marsha L. Dutton, in Coll 57 (1995) [608]–[609]; Daniel M. La Corte, in *Theological Studies* 56 (1995) 399; and Katherine M. TePas, in Cîteaux 45 (1994) 400–403.

42. Bestul, review in *Speculum* 71 (1996) 466.

43. Marsha L. Dutton, "The Invented Sexual History of Aelred of Rievaulx: A Review Article," *The American Benedictine Review* 47 (1996) 432.

Dutton's article (pp. 414–32) contains a much more detailed history of the scholarship on this question than I have presented.

44. In CSQ 29 (1994) 121–96.

45. Dutton, "Invented Sexual History," p. 432.

46. Dutton, "Aelred...on...Sex," p. 196.

2. Adam's Wondrous Dignity

1. Nat M 24.17; CCCM 2A:194; CF 58:332–33.

2. Kal Nov 78.1; CCCM 2B:302.

3. Cler 28.17; CCCM 2A:233; CF 58:387. See Gerd Fösges, *Das Menschenbild bei Aelred von Rievaulx,* Münsteraner Theologische Abhandlungen 29 (Altenberg: Oros Verlag, 1994), pp. 61–65, 71–73.

4. Oner 16; PL 195:423D.

5. See Oner 2; PL 195:363AB.

6. See Kal Nov 78.18; CCCM 2B:307–8.

7. Spec car 1.3.8; CCCM 1:16; CF 17:91.

8. Asspt 20.4; CCCM 2A:155; CF 58:276.

9. Spec car 3.22.52; CCCM 1:130; CF 17:256.

10. Anima 1.28; CCCM 1:693; CF 22:48.

11. Adv 2.24; CCCM 2A:22; CF 58:85.

12. See Adv 2.21; CCCM 2A:22; CF 58:84.

13. See Anima 1.63; CCCM 1:705; CF 22:68.

14. See Anima 1.40; CCCM 1:696; CF 22:54 and Anima 2.60; CCCM 1:730; CF 22:108.

15. Spir amic 1.57–58; CCCM 1:298–99; CF 5:63.

16. Caroline Walker Bynum's groundbreaking studies of the body in medieval spirituality are full of references to the contributions of Bernard of Clairvaux, in part based on my own studies of Bernard on the body, but they contain little on Aelred's teaching. See Bynum's *The Resurrection of the Body in Western Christianity, 200–1336,* Lectures on the History of Religions Sponsored by the American Council of Learned Societies, New Series 15 (New York: Columbia University Press, 1995); for Bernard, see pp. 164–66 and other references listed in the index; for Aelred, see p. 210. See too Bynum's *Fragmentation and Redemption: Essays on Gender and the Human Body in*

Medieval Religion (New York: Zone Books, 1991); for Bernard, see pp. 256–59 and other references listed in the index; for Aelred, see pp. 158–59. Although Bynum cites my work from an unpublished paper, its content is accessible in my *The Spiritual Teachings of Bernard of Clairvaux*, An Intellectual History of the Early Cistercian Order [1], CS 125 (Kalamazoo, Michigan: Cistercian Publications, 1991, reprinted 2004), pp. 13–17, 23–26, and 31–38. A reading of Aelred's teaching on the body, which sometimes differs from my own reading, can be found in Fösges, *Das Menschenbild*, pp. 150–90.

17. See Anima 1.10; CCCM 1:687; CF 22:39.

18. See Anima 2.18; CCCM 1:713; CF 22:81.

19. Anima 1.17; CCCM 1:690; CF 22:43.

20. See Anima 1.25–26; CCCM 1:692; CF 22:47.

21. Anima 1.19; CCCM 1:691; CF 22:45. Aelred is quoting Augustine's *De Genesi ad litteram* 7.13.20.

22. Ie 53.18; CCCM 2B:63.

23. Nat M 75.47; CCCM 2B:281.

24. Anima 1.13; CCCM 1:688; CF 22:41.

25. Pasc 12.12; CCCM 2A:100; CF 58:197.

26. See Asc 13.5; CCCM 2A:105–6; CF 58:206.

27. App 31.6; CCCM 2A:251–52.

28. Anima 1.61; CCCM 1:704; CF 22:66–67.

29. Pasc 41.7–8; CCCM 2A:325–26. See Inst incl 3.33; CCCM 1:678; CF 2:98.

30. See Asspt 21.13; CCCM 2A:167; CF 58:293.

31. Anima 3.7; CCCM 1:734; CF 22:114–15.

32. Asc 13.36; CCCM 2A:113; CF 58:216.

33. Spec car 1.34.111; CCCM 1:62; CF 17:156.

34. OS 46.13; CCCM 2A:369.

35. See Anima 1.30–31; CCCM 1:694; CF 22:49.

36. Anima 1.10; CCCM 1:687; CF 22:39.

37. See Anima 2.11; CCCM 1:710; CF 22:76.

38. Anima 1.10; CCCM 1:687; CF 22:39. See Fösges, *Das Menschenbild*, pp. 137–46.

39. Anima 1.11; CCCM 1:687–88; CF 22:39–40.

40. Pent 67.11–12; CCCM 2B:184.

41. Pent 67.9; CCCM 2B:183. This sermon receives a more extended

commentary in Philippe Nouzille, *Expérience de Dieu et théologie monastique au XIIe siècle: Étude sur les sermons d'Aelred de Rievaulx* (Paris: Les Éditions du Cerf, 1999), pp. 96–100.

42. Anima 2.61; CCCM 1:730; CF 22:109.

43. See Anima 1.5; CCCM 1:686; CF 22:37.

44. See Anima 2.16; CCCM 1:711–12; CF 22:79.

45. Anima 2.1; CCCM 1:707; CF 22:71.

46. Anima 1.43; CCCM 1:697–98; CF 22:56.

47. Syn pres 64.12; CCCM 2B:165. Emphasis mine.

48. Nat M 75.13; CCCM 2B:272.

49. Spec car 1.3.9; CCCM 1:16; CF 17:91–92.

50. See Anima 2.18; CCCM 1:713; CF 22:81.

51. Anima 2.18–19; CCCM 1:713; CF 22:81.

52. See Anima 1.13; CCCM 1:688–89; CF 22:41.

53. The preceding pages contain many instances of this. For another example, see Pent 76.10; CCCM 2B:183.

54. See Pur 32.3; CCCM 2A:260.

55. Nat M 75.9; CCCM 2B:271.

56. Anima 2.14; CCCM 1:711; CF 22:78.

57. Palm 35.10; CCCM 2A:289.

58. Nat 3.20; CCCM 2A:31; CF 58:97.

59. Anima 1.29; CCCM 1:693; CF 22:48–49.

60. See Anima 1.28; CCCM 1:693; CF 22:48.

61. Anima 1.55; CCCM 1:702; CF 22:63.

62. Anima 2.20; CCCM 1:714; CF 22:82.

63. Anima 2.15; CCCM 1:711; CF 22:78.

64. Anima 1.31; CCCM 1:694; CF 22:50.

65. Pur 34.18; CCCM 2A:283.

66. See Anima 2.18; CCCM 1:712–13; CF 22:80–81.

67. Anima 1.38; CCCM 1:696; CF 22:53.

68. Spec car 2.18.53; CCCM 1:91; CF 17:200.

69. Pent 67.10; CCCM 2B:184.

70. Anima 2.25; CCCM 1:715; CF 22:85.

71. Anima 2.27; CCCM 1:716; CF 22:87.

72. Anima 2.29; CCCM 1:717; CF 22:88.

73. See Anima 2.35; CCCM 1:720; CF 22:92.

74. Spec car 3.8.22; CCCM 1:115; CF 17:235–36.

75. Spec car 1.10.29; CCCM 1:24; CF 17:103.

76. Spec car 3.17.40; CCCM 1:124; CF 17:248.

77. Spec car 3.17.40; CCCM 1:124; CF 17:248.

78. Spec car 3.17.40; CCCM 1:124; CF 17:248.

79. See PP 70.32; CCCM 2B:216.

80. See Anima 2.49; CCCM 1:724; CF 22:99–100.

81. Anima 2.15; CCCM 1:711; CF 22:78.

82. Anima 3.9; CCCM 1:735; CF 22:116.

83. See Anima 3.9 (CCCM 1:735; CF 22:116), Pent 67.9–10 (CCCM 2B:183), and Oner 20 (PL 195:440D).

84. See Anima 3.10; CCCM 1:735; CF 22:116–17.

85. Anima 2.12; CCCM 1:710; CF 22:77.

86. Augustine's great influence on Aelred's treatise *On the Soul* is indicated by the myriad footnote references to Augustine in the critical edition by C. H. Talbot: CCCM 1:685–754. In Talbot's translation of this treatise, he lists twenty-one of Augustine's works as the sources of, or as exhibiting affinity with, Aelred's thought on the soul. See CF 22:153.

87. Although this is a principal theme of Augustine's treatise, Elizabeth Connor offers the following specific locations: *De Trinitate* 14.8.11, 10.11.17, and 11.1.1. See her "Saint Bernard's Three Steps of Truth and Saint Aelred of Rievaulx's Three Loves," in John R. Sommerfeldt, ed., *Bernardus Magister: Papers Presented at the Nonacentenary Celebration of the Birth of Saint Bernard of Clairvaux, Kalamazoo, Michigan, Sponsored by the Institute of Cistercian Studies, Western Michigan University, 10–13 May 1990*, CS 135 (Kalamazoo, Michigan: Cistercian Publications; Saint-Nicolas-lès-Cîteaux: Cîteaux: Commentarii Cistercienses, 1992), p. 227 and n. 6.

88. The rendering of *affectus* as "affection" is inadequate since *affectus* "implies more than temporary, unstable impulses." See Brian Patrick McGuire, *Friendship & Community: The Monastic Experience, 350–1250*, CS 95 (Kalamazoo, Michigan: Cistercian Publications Inc., 1988), p. 298. On the other hand, Katherine M. Yohe, while acknowledging that "it is difficult to find an English equivalent of *affectus* that fits all contexts," opts for "affection," precisely "because it carries the connotation of warmth and delight that belong to Aelred's meaning." See "Adhering to a Friend in the Spirit of Christ," CSQ 33 (1998) 33, n. 16. The following section is drawn

from an earlier treatment of the question in my "The Roots of Aelred's Spirituality: Cosmology and Anthropology," CSQ 38 (2003) 19–26.

89. Spec car 3.11.31; CCCM 1:119; CF 17:241. The word translated as "delightful" is *dulcis*. The CF 17 translator, Elizabeth Connor, quite properly, I think, avoids the more obvious "sweet." See McGuire, *Friendship & Community*, p. 299.

90. Yp 51.5; CCCM 2B:41.

91. Ann dom 57.14; CCCM 2B:102.

92. See Spec car 1.34.112; CCCM 1:63; CF 17:157.

93. Spec car 2.14.35; CCCM 1:83; CF 17:188.

94. Inst incl 2.22; CCCM 1:655; CF 2:69. Aelred clearly approves of the wrath of King Edmund of England at the invasions of the Danes. See Gen Angl; PL 195:732B.

95. Spec car 3.11.31; CCCM 1:119; CF 17:241. See James McEvoy, "Les 'affectus' et la mesure de la raison dans le Livre III du 'Miroir,'" Coll 55 (1993) 110–25, especially pp. 117–19.

96. Spec car 3.15.38; CCCM 1:122–23; CF 17:246.

97. Spec car 3.15.38; CCCM 1:123; CF 17:246.

98. See above, p. 13.

99. Spec car 3.14.36; CCCM 1:121; CF 17:244.

100. See Spec car 3.14.36–37; CCCM 1:122; CF 17:244–45.

101. Spec car 3.14.37; CCCM 1:122; CF 17:245–46.

102. Anima 1.17–18; CCCM 1:690; CF 22:43–44.

103. Spec car 3.13.35; CCCM 1:121; CF 17:243.

104. Spec car 3.12.33; CCCM 1:120; CF 17:242.

105. Spec car 3.11.31; CCCM 1:119; CF 17:241.

106. SS Hag, prologus; Raine, p. 174.

107. Ann dom 58.20; CCCM 2B:112.

108. Anima 1.49; CCCM 1:699; CF 22:59. See Anima 1.45 (CCCM 1:698; CF 22:57) for Aelred's source for this position in Augustine.

109. Anima 1.4; CCCM 1:686; CF 22:37.

110. Anima 1.44; CCCM 1:698; CF 22:56.

111. Nat PP 18.18; CCCM 2A:144; CF 58:259–60.

112. Asc 65.5; CCCM 2B:171.

113. Nat 49.3–5; CCCM 2B:22–23.

114. Nat 49.5; CCCM 2B:23.

3. Adam's Fall and Restoration

1. Spec car 1.4.11; CCCM 1:17; CF 17:92–93.

2. See Spec car 1.4.12; CCCM 1:17; CF 17:93.

3. See Iesu 1.3 (CCCM 1:251–52; CF 2:6–7), Oner 8 (PL 195:391A), and Spec car 1.2.6 (CCCM 1:15; CF 17:90–91).

4. Pent 67.14; CCCM 2B:185.

5. Pent 67.14; CCCM 2B:185.

6. Pent 67.14; CCCM 2B:185.

7. Pent 67.15; CCCM 2B:185.

8. Pent 67.16; CCCM 2B:185.

9. Nat 49.6; CCCM 2B:23.

10. Nat 49.6; CCCM 2B:23–24.

11. See below, pp. 41–43.

12. See above, pp. 20–21.

13. See Anima 2.23; CCCM 1:714; CF 22:84.

14. Nat 49.7; CCCM 2B:24.

15. Oner 2; PL 195:363BC.

16. See Oner 11; PL 195:404C.

17. Nat JB 43.17; CCCM 2A:340.

18. Anima 2.34; CCCM 1:719; CF 22:91–92.

19. See Spec car 1.12.37; CCCM 1:27; CF 17:107.

20. See Spec car 1.12.37; CCCM 1:27; CF 17:107–8.

21. See Oner 6; PL 195:381AB.

22. See Anima 2.27; CCCM 1:716; CF 22:86–87.

23. See Anima 2.28; CCCM 1:717; CF 22:87.

24. Asspt 21.4; CCCM 2A:165–66; CF 58:290.

25. See Anima 2.29; CCCM 1:717; CF 22:88.

26. OS 26.24; CCCM 2A:215; CF 58:361–62.

27. Spec car 1.8.25; CCCM 1:22; CF 17:100.

28. See Anima 2.13; CCCM 1:711; CF 22:77.

29. See Spec car 1.5.16; CCCM 1:19; CF 17:96.

30. See Oner 10 (PL 195:397C) and Oner 30 (PL 195:489B).

31. See Oner 29; PL 195:483BC.

32. Spec car 3.11.32; CCCM 1:119–20; CF 17:241–42. Whether Aelred's example is indeed a case of *spiritual* attachment gone wrong is irrelevant. He thinks it is.

33. See above, p. 24.

34. Spec car 3.12.34; CCCM 1:121; CF 17:243.

35. Spec car 3.15.38; CCCM 1:123; CF 17:246–47.

36. See Adv 47.9; CCCM 2B:5.

37. See Adv 47.22; CCCM 2B:9.

38. See Spec car 3.40.111; CCCM 1:160; CF 17:300.

39. Oner 16; PL 195:423B.

40. See PP 70.32; CCCM 2B:217.

41. Syn pres 64.18; CCCM 2B:167. See Kal Nov 78.28; CCCM 2B:310–11.

42. See Anima 2.20; CCCM 1:713; CF 22:82.

43. Anima 2.60; CCCM 1:730; CF 22:108–9.

44. Ie 52.13; CCCM 2B:52. See Ann dom 57.6 (CCCM 2B:100) and Asc 13.1 (CCCM 2A:105; CF 58:205).

45. Pasc 12.13; CCCM 2A:100; CF 58:198.

46. Spec car 1.9.27; CCCM 1:23; CF 17:101–2.

47. See, for example, Anima 2.20; CCCM 1:713; CF 22:82.

48. Palm 35.10; CCCM 2A:289.

49. See Anima 1.18; CCCM 1:690; CF 22:44.

50. See PP 70.32; CCCM 2B:217.

51. OS 26.34; CCCM 2A:217; CF 58:364.

52. Inst incl 3.31; CCCM 1:669; CF 2:88.

53. One must "concede to the body what is owed to it by nature." Spec car 3.37.98; CCCM 1:153; CF 17:290.

54. See Spec car 3.23.53; CCCM 1:130; CF 17:257.

55. Ie 52.7; CCCM 2B:50.

56. Ben 55.2; CCCM 2B:81.

57. Spec car 3.8.22; CCCM 1:115; CF 17:235.

58. Nat Ben 8.4; CCCM 2A:65–66; CF 58:148.

59. Spec car 2.5.10; CCCM 1:71; CF 17:170.

60. See Oner 27; PL 195:472D–73A.

61. See Oner 25; PL 195:462C. See too Daniel M. La Corte, "Aelred of Rievaulx's Doctrine of Grace and Its Role in the *Reformatio* of the Soul," in E. Rozanne Elder, ed., *Praise No Less than Charity: Studies in Honor of M. Chrysogonus Waddell, Monk of Gethsemani Abbey,* CS 193 (Kalamazoo, Michigan: Cistercian Publications, 2002), pp. 175–96.

62. See, for example, Pasc 12.5–7; CCCM 2A:99; CF 58:195–96. See too Nat 30.11; CCCM 2A:246.

63. OS 46.17; CCCM 2A:370.

64. Inst incl 3.32; CCCM 1:675; CF 2:95.

65. Oner 1.2; PL 184:819.

66. See above, p. 31.

67. See, for example, Anima 2.52; CCCM 1:726; CF 22:102.

68. Oner 2; PL 195:366A. See, too, Oner 27; PL 195:475.

69. Nat JB 14.10; CCCM 2A:116; CF 58:221.

70. Spec car 3.3.6; CCCM 1:108; CF 17:225.

71. Spec car 1.11.31; CCCM 1:25; CF 17:104. For a discussion of Aelred's teaching on prevenient grace and the Apostle Paul's influence on it, see Elizabeth Connor, "Monastic Profession According to Aelred of Rievaulx," in Francis R. Swietek and John R. Sommerfeldt, eds., Studiosorum Speculum: *Studies in Honor of Louis J. Lekai, O.Cist.*, CS 141 (Kalamazoo, Michigan: Cistercian Publications, 1993), p. 59.

72. Spec car 1.12.36; CCCM 1:27; CF 17:107.

73. Inst incl 3.31; CCCM 1:665; CF 2:83. Writing of the woman who washed Jesus' feet at the banquet before his death, Marsha Dutton says: "Aelred's epithet for her...is 'that blessed sinner,' *illa beatissima peccatrice.* There is no suggestion that the woman has asked forgiveness nor that she is less guilty than she is accused of being, only that she is happy in Christ's blessing." See Dutton (writing as Marsha D. Stuckey), "A Prodigal Writes Home: Aelred of Rievaulx's *De institutione inclusarum,*" in E. Rozanne Elder, ed., *Heaven on Earth: Studies in Medieval Cistercian History, IX,* CS 68 (Kalamazoo, Michigan: Cistercian Publications, 1983), p. 39.

74. Inst incl 3.31; CCCM 1:666; CF 2:84.

75. Spec car 1.12.38; CCCM 1:28; CF 17:108.

76. Nat Ben 37.5; CCCM 2A:301.

77. Spec car 1.10.28; CCCM 1:23–24; CF 17:102–3.

78. Spec car 1.10.28; CCCM 1:24; CF 17:103.

79. Spec car 1.11.32; CCCM 1:25; CF 17:105.

80. Spec car 1.11.33; CCCM 1:26; CF 17:105.

81. Spec car 1.11.33; CCCM 1:26; CF 17:105.

82. Spec car 1.11.34; CCCM 1:26; CF 17:106.

83. See Anima 2.51; CCCM 1:725; CF 22:101.

84. Spec car 1.11.31; CCCM 1:25; CF 17:104.

85. Pent 68.24; CCCM 2B:199.

4. Humility: The Perfection of the Intellect

1. See Anima 2.18–19; CCCM 1:713; CF 22:81.

2. Oner 12; PL 195:406B.

3. See above, pp. 30–31.

4. See above, p. 28.

5. Spec car 1.22.63; CCCM 1:39; CF 17:123.

6. Spec car 1.22.64; CCCM 1:39; CF 17:123–24.

7. Pasc 11.15; CCCM 2A:92; CF 58:186.

8. Ann dom 59.8; CCCM 2B:120. See Nat 49.5; CCCM 2B:23.

9. OS 25.7; CCCM 2A:205; CF 58:348.

10. Ben 54.34; CCCM 2B:78.

11. Asspt 21.33; CCCM 2A:171–72; CF 58:299–300.

12. See Oner 13; PL 195:410C.

13. Oner 22; PL 195:449C. See Oner 12; PL 195:405D–406A.

14. See Adv 47.28; CCCM 2B:11.

15. See Oner 13; PL 195:410D–11A.

16. See OS 27.12–13; CCCM 2A:224–25; CF 58:374.

17. Ben 55.14; CCCM 2B:85.

18. See Pur 34.19 (CCCM 2A:283) and Oner 9 (PL 195:395B).

19. Oner 22; PL 195:451C.

20. Iesu 2.12; CCCM 1:259; CF 2:16.

21. See above, p. 35.

22. Asspt 21.27; CCCM 2A:170; CF 58:297–98.

23. Pur 33.4; CCCM 2A:267.

24. Spec car 1.8.24; CCCM 1:22; CF 17:100.

25. Spec car 2.1.3; CCCM 1:67; CF 17:164.

26. Inst incl 3.30; CCCM 1:664; CF 2:81.

27. Inst incl 3.29; CCCM 1:664; CF 2:81.

28. Inst incl 3.32; CCCM 1:676; CF 2:96.

29. Asc 13.38; CCCM 2A:113; CF 58:216.

30. See my "Images of Visitation: The Vocabulary of Contemplation in Aelred of Rievaulx' *Mirror of Love*, Book II," in *Erudition*, p. 162. See p. 167, n. 6, for the specific location of these references. For additional examples, see my "The Vocabulary of Contemplation in Aelred of Rievaulx' *On Jesus at the Age of Twelve, A Rule of Life for a Recluse,* and *On Spiritual Friendship*," in *Heaven on Earth*, pp. 73–77 and 81–83; "The Vocabulary of

Contemplation in Aelred of Rievaulx' *Mirror of Love*, Book I," in E. Rozanne Elder, ed., *Goad and Nail: Studies in Medieval Cistercian History, X*, CS 84 (Kalamazoo, Michigan: Cistercian Publications, 1985), pp. 242–45; and "The Rape of the Soul: The Vocabulary of Contemplation in Aelred of Rievaulx' *Mirror of Love*, Book III," in *Erudition*, p. 172.

31. For Aelred's use of the imagination in meditation, see Marie A. Mayeski, "A Twelfth-Century View of the Imagination: Aelred of Rievaulx," in E. Rozanne Elder, ed., *Noble Piety and Reformed Monasticism: Studies in Medieval Cistercian History, VII*, CS 65 (Kalamazoo, Michigan: Cistercian Publications Inc., 1981), pp. 125–26.

32. See above, p. 21, quoting Pent 67.9 (CCCM 2B:183) and Oner 20 (PL 195:440D).

33. See Ann 39.1; CCCM 2A:312.

34. See Ben 55.3 and 11; CCCM 2B:81–82 and 84.

35. Inst incl 1.11; CCCM 1:648; CF 2:59.

36. See Ben 54.30; CCCM 2B:77.

37. Spec car 3.3.6; CCCM 1:107–8; CF 17:225.

38. Spec car 2.26.78; CCCM 1:103; CF 17:218. See Nat 3.21; CCCM 2A:31–32; CF 58:98.

39. See Orat past 8; CCCM 1:762; CF 2:116 or CSQ 38:307; CSQ 37:465.

40. Iesu 3.24; CCCM 1:271; CF 2:31–32.

41. Spec car 3.3.6; CCCM 1:108; CF 17:225.

42. Walter Daniel, *Vita Aelredi* 10; Powicke, p. 19; CF 57:103.

43. Pent 57.7; CCCM 2B:182–83. See Iesu 3.25; CCCM 1:271–72; CF 2:32–33.

44. Spec car 1.21.59; CCCM 1:37; CF 17:121.

45. OS 76.22; CCCM 2B:291. For an excellent survey of Aelred's attitude toward, and use of, Scripture, see Amédée Hallier, *The Monastic Theology of Aelred of Rievaulx: An Experiential Theology*, trans. Columban Heaney, CS 2 (Shannon, Ireland: Irish University Press, 1969), pp. 86–101.

46. Syn pres 64.14; CCCM 2B:166.

47. App 4.32; CCCM 2A:44; CF 58:116.

48. Asc 13.23; CCCM 2A:110; CF 58:212.

49. Nat M 75.51; CCCM 2B:283.

50. See Nat M 22.9; CCCM 2A:178; CF 58:309.

51. Oner 27; PL 195:476B. See also Ben 55.3; CCCM 2B:81–82.

52. Oner 2; PL 195:363C.

53. Pent 42.10; CCCM 2A:334.

54. Iesu 1.1; CCCM 1:249; CF 2:3.

55. Iesu 1.1; CCCM 1:249–50; CF 2:4.

56. See Iesu 1.2; CCCM 1:250; CF 2:5.

57. See Iesu 1.3–11; CCCM 1:251–58; CF 2:5–14.

58. Iesu 2.14; CCCM 1:260; CF 2:17–18.

59. "Secundum moralem sensum" (CCCM 1:265). The title of this and the other two sections the editor, Anselme Hoste, has placed in brackets, to indicate that these traditional (but accurate) divisions are so titled in the margin of only one manuscript. See CCCM 1:249, note *Titulus*.

60. See Iesu 3.20; CCCM 1:266–67; CF 2:26–27.

61. See Iesu 3.19; CCCM 1:265–66; CF 2:25–26.

62. Iesu 3.32; CCCM 1:278; CF 2:39. On the difference between Aelred's attempts at "spiritual understanding" of Scripture and the "strictly scientific exegesis of Scripture or even a purely objective intellectual delineation of the Scriptural theological themes . . . ," see Odo Brooke, "Monastic Theology and St Aelred," in his *Studies in Monastic Theology,* CS 37 (Kalamazoo, Michigan: Cistercian Publications, 1980), p. 222.

63. Pent 67.2; CCCM 2B:181.

64. Iesu 1.9; CCCM 1:257; CF 2:12.

65. See RB 48. For an excellent description of *lectio divina,* see Paul Diemer, "St Ailred of Rievaulx (d. 1167)," in D. H. Farmer, ed., *Benedict's Disciples* (Leominster, Herefordshire: Fowler Wright Books Ltd, 1980), p. 182. See too Nouzille, pp. 124–30.

66. Inst incl 3.31; CCCM 1:668; CF 2:86.

67. See Pasc 11.28; CCCM 2A:95; CF 58:190–91.

68. Oner 32; PL 195:496CD.

69. Ie 52.4 (CCCM 2B:49).

70. Nat M 23.3; CCCM 2A:184; CF 58:319. See Spec car 2.1.3; CCCM 1:67; CF 17:164.

71. Pur 5.19; CCCM 2A:50; CF 58:125.

72. See Pur 33.31 (CCCM 2A:273–74), Pur 33.21 (CCCM 2A:271–72), and Ie 52.14 (CCCM 2B:52).

73. Spec car 2.14.35; CCCM 1:82–83; CF 17:188.

74. See Palm 35.15; CCCM 2A:291.

75. Oner 9; PL 195:394A.

76. Oner 13; PL 195:410BC. See Hallier, *Monastic Theology,* pp. 157–60, for a discussion of Aelred's meditations on death and the "things of eternity" (p. 158).

77. See Cler 28.17; CCCM 2A:233–34; CF 58:387.

78. Nat M 75.29; CCCM 2B:277.

79. Iesu 3.28; CCCM 1:274; CF 2:35.

80. Iesu 3.28; CCCM 1:275; CF 2:35–36.

81. See Adv 47.5; CCCM 2B:4.

82. Pasc 11.33; CCCM 2A:96; CF 58:192.

83. Inst incl 3.31; CCCM 1:669; CF 2:88. For the relationship between Christ's divinity and his humanity, see Dutton, "Christ Our Mother: Aelred's Iconography for Contemplative Union," in *Goad and Nail,* pp. 25–40; "Eat, Drink, and Be Merry: The Eucharistic Spirituality of the Cistercian Fathers," in *Erudition,* pp. 17–20; and "Intimacy and Imitation: The Humanity of Christ in Cistercian Spirituality," in *Erudition,* pp. 38–39 and 47–48. See too Inst incl 3.31; CCCM 1:668; CF 2:87.

84. Adv 1.5; CCCM 2A:4; CF 58:58.

85. Inst incl 3.31; CCCM 1:673; CF 2:92.

86. See Spec car 1.7.22; CCCM 1:21; CF 17:98–99.

87. Asspt 20.4; CCCM 2A:156; CF 58:276.

88. Oner 29; PL 195:483D.

5. Love: The Perfection of the Will

1. Asspt 19.13; CCCM 2A:149; CF 58:267.

2. Spec car 2.1.1; CCCM 1:66; CF 17:163.

3. Ben 55.14; CCCM 2B:85.

4. Spec car 1.1.3; CCCM 1:14; CF 17:89.

5. Pent 68.3–4; CCCM 2B:191–92.

6. *Epistola ad G. Lundoniensem episcopum;* PL 195:361–62. For the Stoic origin of Aelred's thought on love as the basis for universal order, see Charles Dumont, "Aelred of Rievaulx's *Spiritual Friendship,*" in *Cistercian Ideals and Reality,* p. 189.

7. See Pent 68.4; CCCM 2B:192.

8. See Spec car 2.18.53; CCCM 1:91; CF 17:200.

9. The obvious translation of *caritas* would be "charity," but I have

avoided this because "charity" carries with it connotations of alms-giving, which is not at all what Aelred means to convey. Similarly, I have not translated *cupiditas* as "cupidity," because Aelred's *cupiditas* does not focus on sexual activity, as the English word often seems to do. Instead, I have followed Elizabeth Connor's excellent translation of *The Mirror of Love* (CF 17) in rendering *cupiditas* as "self-centered love" or as "self-centeredness." Aelred often uses *amor* and *dilectio,* which for him seem to be morally neutral, and so I have translated these simply as "love."

10. Spec car 1.9.27; CCCM 1:23; CF 17:101.

11. Spec car 1.8.26; CCCM 1:23; CF 17:101.

12. Spec car 2.2.5; CCCM 1:68; CF 17:166.

13. Spec car 2.3.6; CCCM 1:68–69; CF 17:167.

14. OS 46.3; CCCM 2A:366.

15. See Spec car 2.21.64; CCCM 1:96; CF 17:207.

16. See Ann 39.19; CCCM 2A:317.

17. Ie 53.21; CCCM 2B:64.

18. PP 70.10; CCCM 2B:211.

19. See PP 18.18; CCCM 2A:143–44; CF 58:259.

20. Spec car 1.16.48; CCCM 1:31–32; CF 17:113.

21. See above, p. 20.

22. See above, p. 21.

23. Spec car 3.20.48; CCCM 1:128; CF 17:253–54. Elizabeth Connor has this insightful comment on the issue: "Chapters 8–13 of Book 2 [of the *Mirror*] are a long development showing that spiritual sweetness is not a criterion for love of God. It is given sometimes to awaken a person to conversion, or, often, to strengthen him in trial either present or to come, and, exceptionally, as a reward for great holiness. But real love is in the will, turning toward God or away. So 'have charity and do what you will' is a valid affirmation, provided 'one understands what one is talking about.'" See "Monastic Profession," in Studiosorum Speculum, p. 70.

24. Nat M 75.25–26; CCCM 2B:276.

25. Spec car 3.10.29; CCCM 1:118; CF 17:240.

26. Spec car 2.18.54; CCCM 1:91–92; CF 17:201.

27. Gen Angl; PL 195:736BC.

28. Inst incl 2.28; CCCM 1:661–62; CF 2:77–78.

29. Oner 9; PL 195:394C.

30. Kal Nov 78.23; CCCM 2B:309.

31. Spir amic 3.69; CCCM 1:331; CF 5:107.

32. Spec car 3.2.3; CCCM 1:106; CF 17:223.

33. Oner 10; PL 195:398C.

34. Spec car 1.33.96; CCCM 1:56; CF 17:146.

35. Spec car 1.34.104; CCCM 1:59–60; CF 17:152.

36. HM 36.11; CCCM 2A:296.

37. Spec car 3.4.7; CCCM 1:108; CF 17:225–26.

38. Spec car 1.19.55; CCCM 1:35; CF 17:118.

39. Spec car 1.1.1; CCCM 1:13; CF 17:87.

40. Spec car 1.1.2; CCCM 1:13; CF 17:88.

41. Adv 1.14; CCCM 2A:6; CF 58:61.

42. Nat PP 15.35–36; CCCM 2A:129–30; CF 58:238–39.

43. HM 36.8; CCCM 2A:295–96.

44. Spec car 3.38.106; CCCM 1:157; CF 17:296.

45. OS 27.8; CCCM 2A:224; CF 58:373.

46. See Spec car 3.2.3; CCCM 1:106–7; CF 17:223.

47. Spec car 3.2.4; CCCM 1:107; CF 17:223–24.

48. Spec car 3.2.4; CCCM 1:107; CF 17:224.

49. Spec car 3.2.5; CCCM 1:107; CF 17:224.

50. Oner 10; PL 195:398D.

51. Nat PP 18.16–17; CCCM 2A:143; CF 58:259.

52. Spec car 1.8.24; CCCM 1:22; CF 17:100.

53. See Nat Ben 6.2 (CCCM 2A:53; CF 58:129) and Spec car 1.1.2 (CCCM 1:13; CF 17:88).

54. Spec car 1.18.52; CCCM 1:33; CF 17:116.

55. Oner 16; PL 195:422C.

56. Spir amic 3.81; CCCM 1:334; CF 5:111–12.

57. Spir amic 3.82; CCCM 1:334; CF 5:112.

6. Friendship and the Perfection of Attachment

1. See Nat Ben 6.2 (CCCM 2A:53; CF 58:129) and Spec car 1.1.2 (CCCM 1:13; CF 17:88).

2. Ann dom 58.13; CCCM 2B:110.

3. Spir amic 1.31; CCCM 1:294; CF 5:58.

4. Spir amic 1.32; CCCM 1:294; CF 5:58.

5. Spir amic 3.2; CCCM 1:317; CF 5:91.

6. Spir amic 3.83; CCCM 1:334–35; CF 5:112.

7. Spir amic 3.51; CCCM 1:327; CF 5:103.

8. See above, pp. 23–24.

9. Spec car 3.23.53; CCCM 1:130; CF 17:257.

10. Spec car 3.23.54; CCCM 1:130; CF 17:257.

11. Spec car 3.23.54; CCCM 1:130–31; CF 17:257–58.

12. Spir amic 2.59; CCCM 1:313; CF 5:84.

13. Yp 51.5; CCCM 2B:41–42.

14. Spir amic 2.57; CCCM 1:313; CF 5:83.

15. Spir amic 3.6; CCCM 1:318; CF 5:92–93. The quotation is from Ambrose, *De officiis* 3.134.

16. Spir amic 3.6; CCCM 1:318; CF 5:93.

17. Spir amic 3.130; CCCM 1:348; CF 5:130.

18. Spir amic 3.68; CCCM 1:330–31; CF 5:107.

19. Spir amic 3.132; CCCM 1:349; CF 5:131.

20. See Spir amic 2.11; CCCM 1:304; CF 5:72. See too Spir amic 3.84; CCCM 1:335; CF 5:113, where the self-revelatory character of friendship is given as a reason for the cautious choice of a friend. More on equality between friends can be found in Spir amic 3.90–91 (CCCM 1:336–37; CF 5: 114–15) and Spir amic 3.96–97 (CCCM 1:339; CF 5:117).

21. See Spir amic 3.88–89; CCCM 1:336; CF 5:114.

22. See Spir amic 3.98–99; CCCM 1:339; CF 5:118–19.

23. Spir amic 3.102; CCCM 1:340; CF 5:119–20.

24. Spir amic 3.101–2; CCCM 1:340; CF 5:119.

25. Spir amic 3.133; CCCM 1:349; CF 5:131.

26. Spir amic 2.61; CCCM 1:313; CF 5:84.

27. Spec car 3.40.112; CCCM 1:161; CF 5:301.

28. Spec car 2.26.75; CCCM 1:102; CF 17:216.

29. Spir amic 3.106–7; CCCM 1:341; CF 5:121.

30. Spir amic 3.107; CCCM 1:341–42; CF 5:121.

31. Spir amic 3.108; CCCM 1:342; CF 5:121–22.

32. Spir amic 3.109; CCCM 1:342; CF 5:122. See also Spir amic 3.109–12; CCCM 1:342–43; CF 5:122–23.

33. Spir amic 3.26; CCCM 1:322; CF 5:97.

34. Spir amic 3.49; CCCM 1:326; CF 5:103.

35. Spec car 3.38.106; CCCM 1:157; CF 17:295–96.

36. Spec car 3.22.52; CCCM 1:130; CF 17:256.

37. See Spir amic 1.54–56; CCCM 1:298; CF 5:62–63.

38. See Spir amic 1.57–58; CCCM 1:298–99; CF 5:63. Quoted above, pp. 11–12.

39. Spir amic 1.51; CCCM 1:297; CF 5:61–62.

40. Spir amic 1.61; CCCM 1:299; CF 5:64.

41. Spir amic 1.60; CCCM 1:299; CF 5:64.

42. Spir amic 3.76; CCCM 1:333; CF 5:110.

43. Spir amic 3.77; CCCM 1:333; CF 5:110.

44. Spir amic 3.81; CCCM 1:334; CF 5:111.

45. Spir amic 1.21; CCCM 1:292; CF 5:55.

46. Spir amic 2.52; CCCM 1:312; CF 5:82.

47. Adv 1.14; CCCM 2A:6; CF 58:61.

48. Nat 49.1; CCCM 2B:22.

49. Spir amic 2.20; CCCM 1:306; CF 5:74. See Spir amic 3.127; CCCM 1:348; CF 5:129.

50. Inst incl 3.31; CCCM 1:667; CF 2:85.

51. Spir amic 2.14; CCCM 1:305; CF 5:73. See Spir amic 3.87; CCCM 1:336; CF 5:114.

52. PP 70.19; CCCM 2B:213.

53. Spir amic 1.69; CCCM 1:301; CF 5:65.

54. Spir amic 1.70; CCCM 1:301; CF 5:66.

55. Spir amic 2.18; CCCM 1:306; CF 5:74. See Spir amic 2.14; CCCM 1:305; CF 5:73.

56. See below, pp. 133–34.

57. See below, pp. 115–16.

58. Spir amic 1.1; CCCM 1:289; CF 5:51.

7. The Path of Virtue

1. Spec car 2.1.3; CCCM 1:66; CF 17:164.

2. Spec car 3.9.25–26; CCCM 1:116–17; CF 17:237–38.

3. Asc 65.17; CCCM 2B:174.

4. Adv 1.30; CCCM 2A:10; CF 58:67.

5. Nat Ben 6.13–14; CCCM 2A:55; CF 58:133.

6. See App 4.31; CCCM 2A:43–44; CF 58:116.

7. Sanct Watt; PL 195:794C.

8. Vita N 4; Historians 5:145; Lives 1:23.

9. PP 71.10; CCCM 2B:223.

10. Pur 33.10; CCCM 2A:269.

11. See Pent 42.9; CCCM 2A:333.

12. Spec car 1.28.79; CCCM 1:46–47; CF 17:133–34.

13. Spec car 1.28.79; CCCM 1:47; CF 17:134–35.

14. Spec car 1.28.81; CCCM 1:48; CF 17:135.

15. Spec car 1.28.81–82; CCCM 1:48; CF 17:135–36.

16. Syn pres 64.11; CCCM 2B:165.

17. Oner 27; PL 195:474CD.

18. Oner 9; PL 195:395D.

19. Oner 20; PL 195:440D–41A.

20. Oner 20; PL 195:441A.

21. PP 70.35; CCCM 2B:217–18. The reference to the first and third hours is a reflection of the Roman—and hence New Testament—computation of time. In this system, the first hour is daybreak, when monks meet to pray "prime," and the third is midmorning, when "tierce" is prayed.

22. Oner 15; PL 195:420D.

23. Sanct Watt; PL 195:795A.

24. Kal Nov 78.27; CCCM 2B:310.

25. PP 70.27; CCCM 2B:215.

26. Kal Nov 78.26; CCCM 2B:310.

27. Oner 25; PL 195:465C.

28. Oner 26; PL 195:469B.

29. See Nat M 30.7; CCCM 2A:245.

30. Oner 10; PL 195:397D and 398B.

31. Nat JB 43.18; CCCM 2A:340.

32. Nat JB 43.18; CCCM 2A:340.

33. Nat JB 43.19; CCCM 2A:341.

34. Nat M 22.21; CCCM 2A:181; CF 58:313.

35. Syn pres 64.21; CCCM 2B:168.

36. Spir amic 1.49; CCCM 1:297; CF 5:61.

37. Ann 39.9; CCCM 2A:314.

38. Syn pres 64.23; CCCM 2B:168–69.

39. See Anima 2.22; CCCM 1:714; CF 22:83.

40. See Ben 55.22; CCCM 2B:87.

41. See Ann 39.10; CCCM 2A:314–15.

42. Ann 39.12; CCCM 2A:315.

43. Spec car 1.34.105; CCCM 1:60; CF 17:152.

44. Spec car 3.21.51; CCCM 1:129; CF 17:255.

45. Ben 55.23; CCCM 2B:87.

46. Oner 29; PL 195:484B. See too Spec car 2.21.64; CCCM 1:96; CF 17:208.

47. Inst incl 2.23; CCCM 1:656; CF 2:70.

48. Spir amic 1.49; CCCM 1:297; CF 5:61.

49. Spec car 3.32.77; CCCM 1:142; CF 17:274.

50. Spec car 3.31.74; CCCM 1:140; CF 17:272.

51. Spec car 3.23.54; CCCM 1:131; CF 17:258. See too Spir amic 2.59; CCCM 1:313; CF 5:84.

52. See above, p. 34.

53. Adv 47.33; CCCM 2B:12.

54. Spec car 3.31.74; CCCM 1:141; CF 17:272.

55. Spec car 2.17.46; CCCM 1:88; CF 17:196. For Aelred, "flesh" is not the body but the misdirected will. See above p. 34.

56. Spec car 3.24.56; CCCM 1:132; CF 17:259.

57. Spec car 1.33.93; CCCM 1:54; CF 17:144.

58. See above, p. 21

59. See Spec car 1.32.91; CCCM 1:53; CF 17:143.

60. App 31.27; CCCM 2A:257.

61. See Spec car 3.31.75; CCCM 1:141; CF 17:272.

62. Oner 22; PL 195:451D.

63. Nat M 22.21; CCCM 2A:181; CF 58:313.

64. Spec car 1.33.97; CCCM 1:56; CF 17:147.

65. Nat M 22.21; CCCM 2A:181; CF 58:313.

66. Spec car 3.21.51; CCCM 1:129; CF 17:255.

67. Ie 52.18; CCCM 2B:54.

68. See Ben 55.25; CCCM 2B:88. Aelred also states that "fortitude is useful against persecutions" in Spec car 3.21.51; CCCM 1:129; CF 17:255. The context of both passages indicates, I think, that by "persecutions" Aelred means "hardships," not the attacks of others.

69. Syn pres 64.21 and 23; CCCM 2B:168.

70. Pasc 61.5; CCCM 2B:140.

71. Palm 35.3; CCCM 2A:287.

72. In Oner 22 (PL 195:452C), Aelred says that "laziness is the enemy of the soul . . . ."

73. Adv 2.42; CCCM 2A:26; CF 58:90.

74. See Yp 51.15; CCCM 2B:45.

75. For an excellent discussion of leisure and tranquility, see Edith Scholl, "The Cistercian Vocabulary: A Proposal," CSQ 27 (1992) 78–84.

76. Anima 1.28; CCCM 1:693; CF 22:48.

77. Ben 54.30; CCCM 2B:77.

78. Nat M 23.17–18; CCCM 2A:188; CF 58:324.

79. See Nat JB 43.28 (CCCM 2A:343) and Inst incl 1.5; CCCM 1:641; CF 2:50.

80. Inst incl 1.5; CCCM 1:641; CF 2:50–51.

81. Inst incl 1.5; CCCM 1:641; CF 2:51.

82. Adv 47.24; CCCM 2B:10.

83. Inst incl 1.7; CCCM 1:643; CF 2:53.

84. Gilbert of Hoyland, *Sermo in Canticum Solomonis* 41.4; PL 184:216D–17A; CF 26:495–96.

85. Gilbert, *Sermo* 41.4; PL 184:217A; CF 26:496.

86. Nat JB 43.6; CCCM 2A:337.

87. Inst incl 3.31; CCCM 1:669; CF 2:87.

88. Iesu 1.17; CCCM 1:264; CF 2:22.

89. Oner 29; PL 195:483B.

90. Nat Ben 6.34; CCCM 2A:60; CF 58:140.

91. Oner 27; PL 195:475C.

92. Spec car 3.32.77; CCCM 1:142; CF 17:274.

93. Ben 54.20; CCCM 2B:74.

94. OS 27.11; CCCM 2A:224; CF 58:374.

95. Spec car 1.22.63; CCCM 1:39; CF 17:123.

96. Oner 22; PL 195:451B.

97. See Spec car 1.24.68; CCCM 1:41; CF 17:126.

98. Ie 53.1; CCCM 2B:58.

99. Nat Ben 6.23; CCCM 2A:57; CF 58:136.

100. See Iesu 3.30; CCCM 1:276; CF 2:37.

101. See Iesu 3.31; CCCM 1:277; CF 2:38.

102. Spec car 3.37.98; CCCM 1:153; CF 17:290.

103. See Ann 39.16 (CCCM 2A:316) and App 31.27 (CCCM 2A:257).

104. Iesu 1.3; CCCM 1:251; CF 2:6.

105. Asc 65.18; CCCM 2B:175.

106. Oner 7; PL 195:387D.

107. See Nat JB 14.20–21; CCCM 2A:119; CF 58:225.

108. See above, p. 34.

109. Asc 65.20; CCCM 2B:175.

110. Oner 8; PL 195:392A.

111. Oner 27; PL 195:475D.

112. See Oner 8; PL 195:391D–92A.

113. Inst incl 2.14; CCCM 1:650; CF 2:62–63.

114. See Asspt 45.28; CCCM 2A:360–61.

115. Inst incl 2.18; CCCM 1:653; CF 2:66–67.

116. Inst incl 2.18; CCCM 1:653–54; CF 2:67.

117. Spir amic 1.63; CCCM 1:300; CF 5:65.

118. See Oner 6; PL 195:382A.

119. See Yp 51.17; CCCM 2B:46.

120. Inst incl 1.9; CCCM 1:645; CF 2:55–56.

121. Inst incl 1.9; CCCM 1:645; CF 2:55.

122. Oner 6; PL 195:383AB.

123. Inst incl 3.31; CCCM 1:666; CF 2:84.

124. Inst incl 1.11; CCCM 1:648; CF 2:59.

8. The Happiness of Perfection

1. Spec car 1.2.6; CCCM 1:15; CF 17:90.

2. Oner 8; PL 195:391CD.

3. See Yp 51.3; CCCM 2B:41.

4. See Spec car 1.2.7; CCCM 1:15; CF 17:91.

5. Spec car 2.19.59; CCCM 1:94; CF 17:205.

6. Kal Nov 78.21; CCCM 2B:308.

7. Oner 8; PL 195:392C.

8. Nat M 24.21; CCCM 24:195; CF 58:334.

9. Nat M 24.21; CCCM 2A:195; CF 58:334–35.

10. Yp 51.14; CCCM 2B:45.

11. Pur 33.19; CCCM 2A:271.

12. OS 26.44; CCCM 2A:220; CF 58:367.

13. OS 46.5; CCCM 2A:367.

14. Spec car 3.31.74; CCCM 1:140; CF 17:272.

15. Nat M 24.23; CCCM 2A:196; CF 58:335.

16. Nat M 24.15–16; CCCM 2A:193–94; CF 58:332.

17. Spec car 1.31.87; CCCM 1:51; CF 17:139–40.

18. See Spec car 1.31.87; CCCM 1:51; CF 17:140.

19. Spec car 1.31.87–88; CCCM 1:51; CF 17:140.

20. Nat Ben 37.16; CCCM 2A:303.

21. Spec car 3.3.6; CCCM 1:108; CF 17:225.

22. Spir amic 3.129; CCCM 1:348; CF 5:130.

23. Oner 16; PL 195:424A.

24. Spec car 1.1.2; CCCM 1:13; CF 17:88.

25. See above, pp. 20–21.

26. See Adv 1.17; CCCM 2A:6–7; CF 58:62.

27. OS 27.14; CCCM 2A:225; CF 58:375.

28. See Nat JB 44.13; CCCM 2A:348.

29. Nat JB 44.14; CCCM 2A:348.

30. Pur 32.19; CCCM 2A:263.

31. Spec car 3.4.11; CCCM 1:110–11; CF 17:229.

32. Thomas X. Davis, speaking of Aelred's teaching on "the harmonious ordering of the inner affections *(affectus)*" says: "Order *(ordo)* among these many and divergent affections brings inner unity, peace, openness, and receptivity to the human spirit that is truly oriented to seeking God." In "Contemplative Action: A Review Essay on Four Articles by Charles Dumont," CSQ 28 (1993) 164.

33. Spir amic 2.38; CCCM 1:309; CF 5:78–79.

34. Nat JB 14.21; CCCM 2A:119; CF 58:225.

35. See Pasc 11.17; CCCM 2A:92; CF 58:187.

36. See Oner 20; PL 195:440CD.

37. Ie 53.25; CCCM 2B:65.

38. Oner 32; PL 195:497ABC.

39. Oner 16; PL 195:424B.

40. See OS 27.20; CCCM 2A:227; CF 58:378.

41. See PP 70.40; CCCM 2B:219.

42. Nat PP 17.21; CCCM 2A:139; CF 58:252.

43. OS 25.3; CCCM 2A:204; CF 58:347.

44. See Nat PP 17.20 (CCCM 2A:138; CF 58:252) and Asspt 21.14 (CCCM 2A:167–68; CF 58:293).

45. Anima 3.46; CCCM 1:752; CF 22:145.

46. Anima 3.47; CCCM 1:752; CF 22:145–46.

47. Nat JB 43.12; CCCM 2A:338.

48. See Nat JB 44.25; CCCM 2A:351.

49. Vita E; PL 195:774C.

50. Asc 65.21; CCCM 2B:176.

51. Vita E; PL 195:775AB.

52. Vita N 11; Historians 5:154; Lives 1:35–36.

53. See above, pp. 77–78.

54. Anima 3.51; CCCM 1:754; CF 22:149.

55. Asc 13.7; CCCM 2A:106; CF 58:207.

56. Inst incl 3.33; CCCM 1:680; CF 2:100.

57. Inst incl 3.33; CCCM 1:680; CF 2:101.

58. Inst incl 3.33; CCCM 1:680; CF 2:101.

59. Adv 78.10–11; CCCM 2B:305.

60. Oner 20; PL 195:443B.

61. Adv 2.8; CCCM 2A:18; CF 58:79.

62. Asspt 45.9; CCCM 2A:354.

63. Asspt 45.34; CCCM 2A:362.

64. Adv 1.12; CCCM 2A:5; CF 58:60–61.

65. Nat M 75.31; CCCM 2B:277.

66. Inst incl 3.33; CCCM 1:681; CF 2:101.

67. Inst incl 3.33; CCCM 1:681; CF 2:101–2.

68. OS 46.9; CCCM 2A:368.

69. See Adv 78.14; CCCM 2B:306–7.

70. See Inst incl 3.33; CCCM 1:681; CF 2:102.

71. See above, p.34.

72. Adv 1.57; CCCM 2A:16; CF 58:76. See too Adv 2.41 (CCCM 2A:26; CF 58:90) and Nat M 75.34; CCCM 2B:278.

73. Spec car 1.20.57; CCCM 1:36; CF 17:120.

74. OS 46.4; CCCM 2A:366–67.

75. See Oner 16; PL 195:422C.

76. See Pent 67.30; CCCM 2B:189.

77. For the condition of the memory in the fallen state, see above, p. 32.

78. Nat M 22.28; CCCM 2A:182–83; CF 58:315–16.

79. Nat M 22.30; CCCM 2A:183; CF 58:316.

80. See Nat JB 44.3; CCCM 2A:345.

81. See above, pp. 70–80.

82. See above, pp. 79–80.

83. Spir amic 3.79; CCCM 1:333; CF 5:111.

84. See above, pp. 74–77.

85. Spir amic 3.80; CCCM 1:333; CF 5:111.

86. See Spir amic 3.134; CCCM 1:349–50; CF 5:131–32.

87. Pasc 12.30; CCCM 2A:104; CF 58:203.

88. Pur 33.18; CCCM 2A:271. In Aelred's *On the Soul*, he treats the status of souls before the last judgment as a matter of opinion. See Anima 3.42; CCCM 1:750; CF 22:142.

89. Inst incl 3.33; CCCM 1:678; CF 2:98.

90. Adv 1.11; CCCM 2A:5; CF 58:60.

91. Pasc 41.11; CCCM 2A:326.

92. App 31.6; CCCM 2A:251.

93. See OS 26.40; CCCM 2A:219.

94. Oner 20; PL 195:443B.

95. Anima 3.7; CCCM 1:734; CF 22:114–15.

96. Pasc 41.8; CCCM 2A:326.

97. See Spec car 1.29.85; CCCM 1:50; CF 17:138. See too Nat JB 14.20–21 (CCCM 2A:119; CF 58:225) and Asspt 21.13 (CCCM 2A:167; CF 58:293).

98. Asspt 45.11; CCCM 2A:355. See too Adv 1.10; CCCM 2A:5; CF 58:60. Both Jesus' transfiguration (see Kal Nov 78.9; CCCM 2B:305) and his physical presence among his disciples (see Asc 13.6; CCCM 2A:106; CF 58:207) show Aelred the value of the human body and the gifts given to it through Jesus' incarnation.

99. Asspt 45.12; CCCM 2A:355.

100. Pasc 41.23; CCCM 2A:330.

101. OS 26.10; CCCM 2A:212; CF 58:357.

102. Spec car 1.22.63; CCCM 1:39; CF 17:123.

103. HM 36.16; CCCM 2A:298.

104. Nat 30.21; CCCM 2A:248.

105. Nat 30.21; CCCM 2A:248.

106. Nat 30.22; CCCM 2A:249.

9. Contemplation

1. PP 71.13; CCCM 2B:224.

2. Asspt 74.5; CCCM 2B:247. It should be pointed out that Aelred's use of *raptus* does not by itself indicate he is speaking of contemplation. See, for example, Pur 34.26; CCCM 2A:285.

3. Nat PP 15.14; CCCM 1:124; CF 58:231.

4. Anima 3.10; CCCM 1:735; CF 22:116.

5. As does the CF 22 translator, C. H. Talbot (see p. 116).

6. OS 26.36; CCCM 2A:218; CF 58:365. One might note that here Aelred uses the word "contemplation" to indicate Paul's rapturous experience.

7. App 31.23–24; CCCM 2A:256.

8. Yp 51.19; CCCM 2B:47. Of course, not all sexual imagery indicates contemplation. See, for example, Ie 53.25; CCCM 2B:65.

9. Ann 39.18; CCCM 2A:317.

10. Spec car 1.1.2; CCCM 1:13; CF 17:88.

11. Pasc 40.16; CCCM 2A:321.

12. Pur 33.34; CCCM 2A:274–75.

13. PP 70.13; CCCM 2B:211–12.

14. Spec car 1.33.94; CCCM 1:55; CF 17:145.

15. Spec car 1.33.94; CCCM 1:55; CF 17:145. See too Asspt 45.9 (CCCM 2A:354), Adv 78.14 (CCCM 2B:306), and Oner 20 (PL 195:443B).

16. Oner 29; PL 195:482D.

17. Oner 29; PL 195:482D.

18. There is a similar difficulty in judging a passage from Oner 19; PL 195:437AB.

19. See above, pp. 45–56.

20. See my "Vocabulary of Contemplation in . . . *Jesus*"; in *Heaven on Earth,* p. 72.

21. See above, p. 45.

22. Inst incl 3.30; CCCM 1:664; CF 2:82. See too Iesu 3.28; CCCM 1:275; CF 2:35.

23. Adv 78.21; CCCM 2B:308.

24. See Adv 1.56 (CCCM 2A:16; CF 58:75) and Adv 2.40 (CCCM 2A:26; CF 58:90).

25. See Inst incl 3.31; CCCM 1:667; CF 2:86.

26. Nat JB 43.23; CCCM 2A:342.

27. Nat JB 43.24; CCCM 2A:342.

28. Inst incl 3.32; CCCM 1:676; CF 2:96. Other examples of "contemplative" language used to express meditation are: Spec car 2.15.38 (CCCM 1:84; CF 17:191) and Oner 29 (PL 195:484A).

29. See, for example, Pur 34.26; CCCM 2A:285.

30. See, for example, Ie 53.25 (CCCM 2B:65), where the spiritual practice is the "fasting" of praise for God.

31. This, and the fact that Aelred immediately turns from this passage to a clear description of the beatific vision (see Inst incl 3.33; CCCM 1:681; CF 2:101–2) has led me to write: "Aelred, I am forced to conclude, simply does not mention the possibility of contemplation to his sister, the recluse. The route laid out in the *Rule* passes from meditation to Beatific Vision, with no foretaste of that Vision in contemplation." In "The Vocabulary of Contemplation in . . . *Jesus*"; in *Heaven on Earth*, p. 75. Marsha Dutton—who surely knows more about *On Reclusion* than I or, I suspect, anyone else—has taken exception to this. In her article "A Prodigal Writes Home" (in *Heaven on Earth*, p. 35), she writes: "Aelred is writing a work of instruction for anchoresses, . . . [that includes] three meditations to assist the anchoress in contemplation. . . . The mystical foretastes of that embrace [of her Bridegroom] in this life and its enjoyment in that to come are the rewards of the anchoress's calling." In her "Christ Our Mother," she quotes my statement about the lack of contemplation in *On Reclusion*, but politely contradicts it: "In fact, however, the second part of *A Rule* is a unified contemplative work; in it Aelred guides the contemplative toward union with God in this life . . . ." (in *Goad and Nail*, p. 23). I agree with this statement. Aelred's work surely promotes a "contemplative" *life*, that is, a life oriented "toward union with God." What it does not describe, I think, is the rapturous, ecstatic experience of God in this life that I have here called "contemplation."

32. It is also not "mystical." "Mystical" signifies for Aelred an allegorical meaning of Scripture and is therefore a kind or level of exegesis. See Iesu 3.19, where Aelred employs the phrase *moribus mystica* (CCCM 1:266, line 9), which CF 2:25 translates as "the hidden things of the spirit." In Book 2 of *The Mirror of Love*, Aelred uses the adjective "mystical" and the adverb "mystically" four times (Spec car 2.6.16 [CCCM 1:74, line 302], 2.15.37

[CCCM 1:84, line 703], 2.23.68 [CCCM 1:98, line 1252], and 2.23.68 [CCCM 1:98, line 1253]). In each case the meaning is "hidden" or "secret."

33. Ann dom 57.21; CCCM 2B:104.

34. Ann dom 57.21; CCCM 2B:104.

35. Ann dom 57.22; CCCM 2B:104.

36. Ann dom 57.23; CCCM 2B:105.

37. Oner 3; PL 195:372A.

38. Oner 3; PL 195:372B.

39. Anima 3.11–12; CCCM 1:735–36; CF 22:117–18.

40. Anima 3.13; CCCM 1:736; CF 22:118–19.

41. Nat M 22.23; CCCM 2A:181; CF 58:314.

42. See Oner 6; PL 195:383CD–84AB.

43. See Hallier, *Monastic Theology*, p. 48.

44. Spec car 2.8.20; CCCM 1:75; CF 17:176–77.

45. See Spec car 2.10.25; CCCM 1:77; CF 17:179.

46. Spec car 2.10.25; CCCM 1:77; CF 17:179–80.

47. Spir amic 2.24; CCCM 1:307; CF 5:76.

48. Spec car 2.11.28; CCCM 1:79; CF 17:182.

49. Spec car 2.19.59; CCCM 1:94; CF 17:205.

50. Spec car 2.12.30; CCCM 1:80; CF 17:183. Much of the preceding paragraph is an adaptation of one I wrote in "Images of Visitation," in *Erudition*, pp. 163–64.

51. I have used almost the same words on p. 164 of "Images of Visitation."

52. Spec car 2.11.28; CCCM 1:78; CF 17:181–82.

53. Spec car 2.12.30; CCCM 1:79; CF 17:183.

54. Spec car 2.13.32; CCCM 1:81; CF 17:185.

55. Spec car 2.15.39; CCCM 1:85; CF 17:192.

56. Spec car 2.12.29; CCCM 1:79; CF 17:182.

57. Spec car 2.13.31; CCCM 1:80; CF 17:184.

58. Spec car 2.19.57; CCCM 1:93; CF 17:203.

59. Spec car 2.19.60; CCCM 1:94; CF 17:205.

60. For the three sorts of sabbaths, see Spec car 3.1.1; CCCM 1:105; CF 17:221. Much of the material in this section has been offered, in a quite different form, in my "Rape of the Soul," in *Erudition*, pp. 169–73. Joseph Molleur has offered a brief analysis of the sabbath theme in "The Notion of

the Three Sabbaths in Aelred's *Mirror of Charity*," CSQ 33 (1998) 211–20. He discusses contemplation on pp. 216–17.

61. See, for example, Spec car 3.2.4; CCCM 1:107; CF 17:224.

62. Spec car 3.1.2; CCCM 1:105; CF 17:221.

63. Spec car 3.2.3; CCCM 1:106; CF 17:223.

64. Spec car 3.6.17; CCCM 1:113; CF 17:232.

65. Spec car 3.6.17; CCCM 1:113; CF 17:232.

66. Spec car 3.6.18; CCCM 1:113; CF 17:232–33.

67. Spec car 3.37.102; CCCM 1:114; CF 17:233–34.

68. Spec car 3.37.102; CCCM 1:156; CF 17:293–94. See too Adv 47.36; CCCM 2B:13.

69. Spir amic 2.26; CCCM 1:307–8; CF 5:76–77.

70. Spir amic 2.27; CCCM 1:308; CF 5:77. I give the reasons for assigning this description to contemplation, rather than the beatific vision, in "Vocabulary of Contemplation in . . . *Jesus*," in *Heaven on Earth*, p. 84.

71. Spir amic 2.61; CCCM 1:313–14; CF 5:84–85.

72. Spir amic 3.127; CCCM 1:348; CF 5:129.

73. Iesu 3.19; CCCM 1:266; CF 2:25. See Thomas Renna, "Cistercians and Bethlehem: A Historical View," in Studiosorum Speculum, pp. 328–29.

74. Iesu 3.19; CCCM 1:226; CF 2:26.

75. Iesu 3.20; CCCM 1:267; CF 2:27.

76. Iesu 3.20; CCCM 1:267–68; CF 2:27–28.

77. Iesu 3.20; CCCM 1:268; CF 2:28.

78. Iesu 3.22; CCCM 1:269–70; CF 2:30.

79. "Sed heu, heu, rara hora et parva mora." Iesu 3.23; CCCM 1:270; CF 2:30. Bernard of Clairvaux uses the same words in describing the brevity of the contemplative experience in *In Cantica canticorum, sermo* 23.15; SBOp 1:148; CF 7:38. See my *The Spiritual Teachings of Bernard of Clairvaux*, p. 220.

80. Iesu 3.24; CCCM 1:271; CF 2:32.

81. Iesu 3.23; CCCM 1:270; CF 2:30.

82. As only one example of many, see Pur 33.19; CCCM 2A:271.

83. See above, p. 130.

84. I have written virtually the same words about Bernard of Clairvaux in *The Spiritual Teachings of Bernard of Clairvaux*, p. 221.

85. See above, pp. 120–21.

86. Oner 3; PL 195:371AB.

87. Walter Daniel, *Epistola ad Mauricium;* Powicke, p. 69; CF 57:149.

88. PP 70.38; CCCM 2B:218.

89. PP 70.38; CCCM 2B:218.

90. PP 70.38; CCCM 2B:218.

Bibliography

I. PRIMARY SOURCES

A. The Works of Aelred of Rievaulx

1. Collections

Aelredi Rievallensis opera omnia, 1, *Opera ascetica.* Ed. A. Hoste and C. H. Talbot. Corpus Christianorum Continuatio Mediaevalis I. Turnholti: Typographi Brepols Editores Pontificii, 1971.

Opera. In J.-P. Migne, ed., *Patrologia latina.* Paris: apud J.-P. Migne editorem, 1841, vol. 32, cols. 1451–52; vol. 158, cols. 785–94; vol. 184, cols. 849–70; vol. 195.

2. Individual Works and Translations

De anima. Ed. C. H. Talbot in *Opera omnia,* vol. 1, pp. 683–754.
Translation: *Dialogue on the Soul.* Trans. C. H. Talbot. Cistercian Fathers 22. Kalamazoo, Michigan: Cistercian Publications, 1981.

De bello standardii. In *Patrologia latina,* vol. 195, cols. 701–12.

Epistola ad G. Lundoniensem episcopum. In *Patrologia latina,* vol. 195, cols. 361–64.

Eulogium Davidis regis Scotorum. In W. M. Metcalfe, ed., *Pinkerton's Lives of the Scottish Saints.* Paisley: Alexander Gardner, 1889, vol. 2, pp. 269–85.

Genealogia regum Anglorum. In *Patrologia latina,* vol. 195, cols. 711–38.

De institutione inclusarum. Ed. C. H. Talbot in *Opera omnia,* vol. 1, pp. 635–82.

>   Translation: *A Rule of Life for a Recluse.* Trans. Mary Paul Macpherson. In *The Works of Aelred of Rievaulx,* I, *Treatises; The Pastoral Prayer.* Cistercian Fathers 2. Spencer, Massachusetts: Cistercian Publications, 1971, pp. 43–102.

De Iesu puero duodenni. Ed. A. Hoste in *Opera omnia,* vol. 1, pp. 246–78.

>   Translation: *The Commentary of the Venerable Aelred, Abbot of Rievaulx, on the Passage from the Gospel: "When Jesus Was Twelve Years Old...."* In *The Works of Aelred of Rievaulx,* I, *Treatises; The Pastoral Prayer.* Cistercian Fathers 2. Spencer, Massachusetts: Cistercian Publications, 1971, pp. 1–39.

Oratio pastoralis. Ed. A. Wilmart in *Opera omnia,* vol. 1, pp. 755–63. Ed. Marsha L. Dutton in *Cistercian Studies Quarterly* 38 (2003) 297–308.

>   Translations: *The Pastoral Prayer.* Trans. R. Penelope Lawson. In *The Works of Aelred of Rievaulx,* I, *Treatises; The Pastoral Prayer.* Cistercian Fathers 2. Spencer, Massachusetts: Cistercian Publications, 1971, pp. 103–18. Trans. Mark DelCoglian, intro. Marsha L. Dutton, in *Cistercian Studies Quarterly* 37 (2002) 453–66.

De sanctimoniali de Wattun. In *Patrologia latina,* vol. 195, cols. 789–96.

De sanctis ecclesiae Haugustaldensis [Hagulstadensis]. In James Raine, ed., *The Priory of Hexham: Its Chronicles, Endowments and Annals,* 1. Surtees Society 44. Durham: Andrews & Co., 1863–1864, pp. 173–203.

Sermones I–XLVI: Collectio Claraevallensis prima et secunda. Ed. Gaetano Raciti. Corpus Christianorum Continuatio Mediaevalis IIA. Turnholti: Typographi Brepols Editores Pontificii, 1989.

>   Partial Translations: Aelred of Rievaulx. *The Liturgical Sermons: The First Clairvaux Collection, Sermons One–Twenty-eight, Advent–All Saints.* Trans. Theodore Berkeley and M. Basil Pennington. Cistercian Fathers 58. Kalamazoo, Spencer, Coalville: Cistercian Publications, 2001. *Sermons on the Feasts of Saint Mary.* Trans. Athanasius Sulavik. In *Cistercian Studies Quarterly* 32 (1997) 37–125.

Sermones XLVII–LXXXIV: Collectio Dunelmensis, Sermo a Matthaeo Rievallensi servatus, Sermones Lincolnienses. Ed. Gaetano Raciti. Corpus Christianorum Continuatio Mediaevalis IIB. Turnhout: Brepols Publishers, 2001.

Sermones inediti b. Aelredi abbatis Rievallensis. Ed. C. H. Talbot. Series scriptorum S. Ordinis Cisterciensis I. Romae: apud Curiam Generalem Sacri Ordinis Cisterciensis, 1952. (Now superseded by Raciti's edition: CCCM 2B.)

Sermones de oneribus. In *Patrologia latina,* vol. 184, cols. 817–28 *[Sermo in adventu Domini],* and vol. 195, cols. 363–500.

De speculo caritatis. Ed. C. H. Talbot. In *Opera omnia,* vol. 1, pp. 5–161.
Translation: *The Mirror of Charity.* Trans. Elizabeth Connor. Cistercian Fathers 17. Kalamazoo, Michigan: Cistercian Publications, 1990.

De spirituali amicitia. Ed. A. Hoste. In *Opera omnia,* vol. 1, pp. 279–350.
Translation: *Spiritual Friendship.* Trans. Mary Eugenia Laker. Cistercian Fathers 5. Washington, DC: Cistercian Publications, 1974.

Vita s. Edwardi regis et confessoris. In *Patrologia latina,* vol. 195, pp. 737–90.
Translation: *The Life of Saint Edward King and Confessor by Blessed Aelred of Rievaulx.* Trans. Jerome Bertram. Guildford, Surrey: St. Edward's Press, 1990.

Vita Niniani Pictorum Australium apostoli. Ed. and trans. Alexander Penrose Forbes, in *Lives of S. Ninian and S. Kentigern.* The Historians of Scotland 5. Edinburgh: Edmonston and Douglas, 1874, pp. 137–57 (text) and 3–26 (translation). The text is also in W. M. Metcalfe, ed., *Pinkerton's Lives of the Scottish Saints.* Paisley: Alexander Gardner, 1889, vol.1, pp. 9–39.

B. Other Primary Sources Cited

Bernard of Clairvaux. *In Cantica canticorum, sermo* 23. In Jean Leclercq et al., eds., *Sancti Bernardi opera.* Romae: Editiones Cisterciensis, 8 vols. in 9, 1957–1977, 1:138–50.

Translation: *The Works of Bernard of Clairvaux,* 3, *On the Song of Songs II.* Trans. Kilian Walsh. Cistercian Fathers 7. Kalamazoo, Michigan: Cistercian Publications, 1976, pp. 25–41.

———. *Epistola ad Aelredum abbatem.* Ed. C. H. Talbot in [Aelred's] *Opera omnia,* vol. 1, pp. 3–4. Also in Jean Leclercq et al., eds., *Sancti Bernardi opera.* Romae: Editiones Cistercienses, 8 vols. in 9, 1957–1977, 8:486–89.
Translation: *A Letter of Bernard, Abbot of Clairvaux, to Abbot Aelred.* Trans. Elizabeth Connor. In Aelred of Rievaulx, *The Mirror of Charity.* Cistercian Fathers 17. Kalamazoo, Michigan: Cistercian Publications, 1990, pp. 69–72.

Gilbert of Hoyland. *Sermo in Canticum Solomonis* 41. In J.-P. Migne, ed., *Patrologia latina.* Paris: apud J.-P. Migne editorem, 1841, vol. 184, cols. 214–19.
Translation: *Sermons on the Song of Songs, III.* Trans. Lawrence C. Braceland. Cistercian Fathers 26. Kalamazoo, Michigan: Cistercian Publications, Inc., 1979, pp. 491–500.

Walter Daniel. *Epistola ad Mauricium.* Ed. F. M. Powicke, with a facing English translation, in *Vita Ailredi Abbatis Rievall'.* London, Edinburgh, Paris, Melbourne, Toronto, New York: Thomas Nelson and Sons Ltd, 1950, reprinted 1963, pp. 66–81. The translation alone has been reprinted in Cistercian Fathers 57. Kalamazoo, Michigan; Spencer, Massachusetts: Cistercian Publications, 1994, pp. 147–58.

———. *Vita Ailredi Abbatis Rievall'.* Ed. F. M. Powicke, with a facing English translation. London, Edinburgh, Paris, Melbourne, Toronto, New York: Thomas Nelson and Sons Ltd, 1950, reprinted 1963, pp. 1–64. The translation alone has been reprinted in Cistercian Fathers 57. Kalamazoo, Michigan; Spencer, Massachusetts: Cistercian Publications, 1994, pp. 89–158.

II. Secondary Sources

Bestul, Thomas H. Review of Brian Patrick McGuire, *Brother and Lover: Aelred of Rievaulx.* New York: Crossroad, 1994. In *Speculum* 71 (1996) 465–67.

Boswell, John Eastburn. *Christianity, Social Tolerance, and Homosexuality: Gay People in Western Europe from the Beginning of the Christian Era to the Fourteenth Century.* Chicago: University of Chicago Press, 1980.

Bouyer, Louis. *The Cistercian Heritage.* Trans. Elizabeth A. Livingstone. London: A. R. Mowbray & Co. Limited, 1958. A translation of *La Spiritualité de Cîteaux.* Paris: au Portulan chez Flammarion, 1955.

Brooke, Odo. "Monastic Theology and St Aelred." In Odo Brooke, *Studies in Monastic Theology.* Cistercian Studies 37. Kalamazoo, Michigan: Cistercian Publications, 1980, pp. 219–25.

Brouette, Émile. "Aelred de Rievaulx." In *Dictionnaire des Auteurs Cisterciens.* Documentation Cistercienne 16. Rochefort, Belgique: Abbaye Notre-Dame de Rochefort, 7 vols., 1975–1979, 1:10–17.

Burton, Janet. "The Estates and Economy of Rievaulx Abbey in Yorkshire." *Cîteaux: Commentarii cistercienses* 49 (1998) 29–94.

Burton, Pierre-André. *Bibliotheca Aelrediana secunda: Un bibliographie cumulative (1962–1996).* Fédération Internationale des Instituts d'Études Médiévales, Textes et Études du Moyen Âge, 7. Louvain-la-Neuve: n.p., 1997.

Bynum, Caroline Walker. *Fragmentation and Redemption: Essays on Gender and the Human Body in Medieval Religion.* New York: Zone Books, 1991.

―――. *The Resurrection of the Body in Western Christianity, 200–1336.* Lectures on the History of Religions Sponsored by the American Council of Learned Societies, New Series 15. New York: Columbia University Press, 1995.

Connor, Elizabeth. "Monastic Profession According to Aelred of Rievaulx." In Francis R. Swietek and John R. Sommerfeldt, eds., Studiosorum Speculum: *Studies in Honor of Louis J. Lekai, O.Cist.* Cistercian Studies 141. Kalamazoo, Michigan: Cistercian Publications, 1993, pp. 53–73.

―――. "Saint Bernard's Three Steps of Truth and Saint Aelred of Rievaulx's Three Loves." In John R. Sommerfeldt, ed., *Bernardus Magister: Papers Presented at the Nonacentenary Celebration of the Birth of Saint Bernard of Clairvaux, Kalamazoo, Michigan, Sponsored by the Institute of Cistercian Studies, Western Michigan University, 10–13 May 1990.* Cistercian Studies 135. Kalamazoo, Michigan: Cistercian Publications; Saint-Nicolas-lès-Cîteaux: Cîteaux: Commentarii Cistercienses, 1992, pp. 225–38.

Davis, Thomas X. "Contemplative Action: A Review Essay on Four Articles by Charles Dumont." *Cistercian Studies Quarterly* 28 (1993) 161–66.

Diemer, Paul. "St Ailred of Rievaulx (d. 1167)." In D. H. Farmer, ed., *Benedict's Disciples.* Leominster, Herefordshire: Fowler Wright Books Ltd, 1980, pp. 175–94.

Dumont, Charles. "Aelred of Rievaulx: His Life and Works." The introduction to Aelred of Rievaulx, *The Mirror of Charity.* Trans. Elizabeth Connor. Cistercian Fathers 17. Kalamazoo, Michigan: Cistercian Publications, 1990, pp. 11–67.

———. "Aelred of Rievaulx's *Spiritual Friendship.*" In John R. Sommerfeldt, ed., *Cistercian Ideals and Reality.* Cistercian Studies 60. Kalamazoo, Michigan: Cistercian Publications, 1978, pp. 187–98.

———. "L'amour fraternel dans la doctrine d'Aelred de Rievaulx." *Collectanea Cisterciensia* 51 (1989) 78–88.

———. "Seeking God in Community According to St Aelred." *Cistercian Studies* 6 (1971) 289–317.

Dutton, Marsha L. "Aelred of Rievaulx on Friendship, Chastity, and Sex: The Sources." *Cistercian Studies Quarterly* 29 (1994) 121–96.

———. "Christ Our Mother: Aelred's Iconography for Contemplative Union." In E. Rozanne Elder, ed., *Goad and Nail: Studies in Medieval Cistercian History, X.* Cistercian Studies 84. Kalamazoo, Michigan: Cistercian Publications, 1985, pp. 21–45.

———. "The Conversion and Vocation of Aelred of Rievaulx: A Historical Hypothesis." In Daniel Williams, ed., *England in the Twelfth Century: Proceedings of the 1988 Harlaxton Symposium.* N.p.: The Boydall Press, 1990, pp. 31–49.

———. "Eat, Drink, and Be Merry: The Eucharistic Spirituality of the Cistercian Fathers." In John R. Sommerfeldt, ed., *Erudition at God's Service: Studies in Medieval Cistercian History, XI.* Cistercian Studies 98. Kalamazoo, Michigan: Cistercian Publications Inc., 1987, pp. 1–31.

———. "Intimacy and Initiation: The Humanity of Christ in Cistercian Spirituality." In John R. Sommerfeldt, ed., *Erudition at God's Service: Studies in Medieval Cistercian History, XI.* Cistercian Studies 98. Kalamazoo, Michigan: Cistercian Publications Inc., 1987, pp. 33–69.

———. "Introduction to Walter Daniels' *Vita Aelredi.*" In Walter Daniel, *The Life of Aelred of Rievaulx.* Cistercian Fathers 57. Kalamazoo, Michigan; Spencer, Massachusetts: Cistercian Publications, 1994, pp. 7–88.

———. "The Invented Sexual History of Aelred of Rievaulx: A Review Article." *The American Benedictine Review* 47 (1996) 414–32.

——— [writing as Marsha D. Stuckey]. "A Prodigal Writes Home: Aelred of Rievaulx's *De institutione inclusarum.*" In E. Rozanne Elder, ed., *Heaven on Earth: Studies in Medieval Cistercian History, IX.* Cistercian Studies 68. Kalamazoo, Michigan: Cistercian Publications, 1983, pp. 35–42.

———. Review of Brian Patrick McGuire, *Brother and Lover: Aelred of Rievaulx.* New York: Crossroad, 1994. In *Collectanea Cisterciensia* 57 (1995) [608]–[609].

Fiske, Adele M. "Aelred of Rievaulx's Idea of Friendship and Love." *Cîteaux: Commentarii cistercienses* 13 (1962) 5–17, 97–132.

———. *Friends and Friendship in the Monastic Tradition,* CIDOC Cuaderno 51. Cuernavaca, Mexico: Centro Intercultural de Documentacion, 1970.

Fösges, Gerd. *Das Menschenbild bei Aelred von Rievaulx.* Münsteraner Theologische Abhandlungen 29. Altenberg: Oros Verlag, 1994.

Glidden, Aelred. "Aelred the Historian: The Account of the Battle of the Standard." In John R. Sommerfeldt, ed., *Erudition at God's Service: Studies in Medieval Cistercian History, XI.* Cistercian Studies 98. Kalamazoo, Michigan: Cistercian Publications Inc., 1987, pp. 175–84.

Hallier, Amédée. *The Monastic Theology of Aelred of Rievaulx: An Experiential Theology.* Trans. Columban Heaney. Cistercian Studies 2. Shannon, Ireland: Irish University Press, 1969. A translation of *Un Éducateur monastique: Aelred de Rievaulx.* Paris: J. Gabalda et Cie, 1959.

Heaney, Columban. "Aelred of Rievaulx: His Relevance to the Post–Vatican II Age." In M. Basil Pennington, ed., *The Cistercian Spirit: A Symposium in Honor of Thomas Merton.* Cistercian Studies 3. Spencer, Massachusetts: Cistercian Publications, 1970, pp. 166–89.

Hoste, Anselm. *Bibliotheca Aelrediana: A Survey of the Manuscripts, Old Catalogues, Editions and Studies Concerning St. Aelred of Rievaulx.* Instrumenta Patristica II. Steenbrugis: in Abbatia Sancti Petri; Hagae Comitis: Martinus Nijhoff, 1962.

Jarrett, Bede. "St. Aelred of Rievaulx (1100–1166)." In Maisie Ward, ed., *The English Way.* New York: Sheed and Ward, 1934, pp. 81–103.

Knowles, David. *The Monastic Order in England: A History of Its Development from the Times of St Dunstan to the Fourth Lateran Council, 943–1216.* Cambridge: Cambridge University Press, 1950.

La Corte, Daniel M. "Aelred of Rievaulx's Doctrine of Grace and Its Role in the *Reformatio* of the Soul." In E. Rozanne Elder, ed., *Praise No Less than Charity: Studies in Honor of M. Chrysogonus Waddell, Monk of Gethsemani Abbey.* Cistercian Studies 193. Kalamazoo, Michigan: Cistercian Publications, 2002, pp. 175–96.

———. Review of Brian Patrick McGuire, *Brother and Lover: Aelred of Rievaulx.* New York: Crossroad, 1994. In *Theological Studies* 56 (1995) 399.

Lekai, Louis J. *The Cistercians: Ideals and Reality.* Kent, Ohio: The Kent State University Press, 1977.

Mayeski, Marie Anne. "A Twelfth-Century View of Imagination: Aelred of Rievaulx." In E. Rozanne Elder, ed., *Noble Piety and Reformed Monasticism: Studies in Medieval Cistercian History, VII.* Cistercian Studies 65. Kalamazoo, Michigan: Cistercian Publications Inc., 1981, pp. 123–29.

McEvoy, James. "Les 'affectus' et la mesure de la raison dans le Livre III du 'Miroir.'" *Collectanea Cisterciensia* 55 (1993) 110–25.

McGinn, Bernard. *The Growth of Mysticism.* The Presence of God: A History of Western Mysticism II. New York: Crossroad, 1994.

McGuire, Brian Patrick. *Brother and Lover: Aelred of Rievaulx.* New York: Crossroad, 1994.

———. *Friendship & Community: The Monastic Experience, 350–1250.* Cistercian Studies 95. Kalamazoo, Michigan: Cistercian Publications Inc., 1988.

Merton, Thomas. "St Aelred and the Cistercians." Ed. Patrick Hart. *Cistercian Studies* 20 (1985) 212–25; 21 (1986) 30–42; 22 (1987) 55–75; 23 (1988) 45–62; 24 (1989) 50–68.

Molleur, Joseph. "The Notion of the Three Sabbaths in Aelred's *Mirror of Charity.*" *Cistercian Studies Quarterly* 33 (1998) 211–20.

Nouzille, Philippe. *Expérience de Dieu et théologie monastique au XIIe siècle: Étude sur les sermons d'Aelred de Rievaulx.* Paris: Les Éditions du Cerf, 1999.

Olsen, Glenn W. "The Gay Middle Ages: A Response to Professor Boswell." *Communio: International Catholic Review* 8 (1981) 119–38.

Powicke, F. M. "Introduction" to *Vita Ailredi abbatis Rievall'.* London, Edinburgh, Paris, Melbourne, Toronto, New York: Thomas Nelson and Sons Ltd, 1950, reprinted 1963, pp. ix–cii.

Renna, Thomas. "Cistercians and Bethlehem: A Historical View." In Francis R. Swietek and John R. Sommerfeldt, eds., Studiosorum Speculum: *Studies in Honor of Louis J. Lekai, O.Cist.* Cistercian Studies 141. Kalamazoo, Michigan: Cistercian Publications, 1993, pp. 321–36.

Roby, Douglas. "Chimaera of the North: The Active Life of Aelred of Rievaulx." In John R. Sommerfeldt, ed., *Cistercian Ideals and Reality.* Cistercian Studies 60. Kalamazoo, Michigan: Cistercian Publications, 1978, pp. 152–69.

———. "Introduction" to Aelred of Rievaulx, *Spiritual Friendship.* Cistercian Fathers 5. Washington, DC: Cistercian Publications, 1974, pp. 1–40.

Scholl, Edith. "The Cistercian Vocabulary: A Proposal." *Cistercian Studies Quarterly* 27 (1992) 77–92.

Sommerfeldt, John R. "Images of Visitation: The Vocabulary of Contemplation in Aelred of Rievaulx' *Mirror of Love,* Book II." In John R. Sommerfeldt, ed., *Erudition at God's Service: Studies in Medieval Cistercian
History, XI.* Cistercian Studies 98. Kalamazoo, Michigan: Cistercian
Publications Inc., 1987, pp. 161–68.

———. "The Rape of the Soul: The Vocabulary of Contemplation in Aelred
of Rievaulx' *Mirror of Love,* Book III." In John R. Sommerfeldt ed., *Erudition at God's Service: Studies in Medieval Cistercian History, XI.* Cistercian Studies 98. Kalamazoo, Michigan: Cistercian Publications Inc.,
1987, pp. 169–74.

———. "The Roots of Aelred's Spirituality: Cosmology and Anthropology."
Cistercian Studies Quarterly 38 (2003) 19–26.

———. *The Spiritual Teachings of Bernard of Clairvaux.* An Intellectual History of the Early Cistercian Order [1]. Cistercian Studies 125. Kalamazoo, Michigan: Cistercian Publications, 1991, reprinted 2004.

———. "The Vocabulary of Contemplation in Aelred of Rievaulx' *On Jesus at
the Age of Twelve, A Rule of Life for a Recluse,* and *On Spiritual
Friendship.*" In E. Rozanne Elder, ed., *Heaven on Earth: Studies in
Medieval Cistercian History, IX.* Cistercian Studies 68. Kalamazoo,
Michigan: Cistercian Publications, 1983, pp. 72–89.

———. "The Vocabulary of Contemplation in Aelred of Rievaulx' *Mirror of
Love,* Book I." In E. Rozanne Elder, ed., *Goad and Nail: Studies in
Medieval Cistercian History, X.* Cistercian Studies 84. Kalamazoo, Michi-
gan: Cistercian Publications, 1985, pp. 241–50.

Squire, Aelred. *Aelred of Rievaulx: A Study.* Cistercian Studies 50. Kalamazoo,
Michigan: Cistercian Publications, 1981. Reprint of London: S.P.C.K.,
1969.

TePas, Katherine. Review of Brian Patrick McGuire, *Brother and Lover:
Aelred of Rievaulx.* New York: Crossroad, 1994. In *Cîteaux: Commentarii cistercienses* 45 (1994) 400–403.

Vanderjagt, Arjo. Review of Brian Patrick McGuire, *Brother and Lover:
Aelred of Rievaulx.* New York: Crossroad, 1994. In *Cistercian Studies
Quarterly* 31 (1996) 225–26.

Vatican II. *Perfectae caritatis* (26 October 1965). Trans. in Austin Flannery,
ed., *Vatican Council II: The Conciliar and Post Conciliar Documents.*
Collegeville, Minnesota: Liturgical Press, 1975, pp. 611–23.

Wright, J. Robert. "Boswell on Homosexuality: A Case Undemonstrated."
Anglican Theological Review 66 (1984) 79–84.

Yohe, Katherine [née TePas]. "Adhering to a Friend in the Spirit of Christ."
Cistercian Studies Quarterly 33 (1998) 29–44.

Index of Persons

181

Index of Topics

Other books in The Newman Press series: